The Cult of the Born-Again Virgin

How Single Women Can Reclaim Their Sexual Power

WENDY KELLER

Health Communications, Inc.
Deerfield Beach, Florida

www.hci-online.com

Library of Congress Cataloging-in-Publication Data

Keller, Wendy, date.
    The cult of the born again virgin : how single women can reclaim their sexual
power / Wendy Keller.
      p. cm.
    Includes bibliographical references and index.
    ISBN 1-55874-696-X
    1. Single women—United States—Sexual behavior. 2. Sexual abstinence—United
States. I. Title.
HQ800.2.K46 1999
306.7'086'52—dc21   99-41515
                                                       CIP

Publisher: Health Communications, Inc.
              3201 S.W. 15th Street
              Deerfield Beach, FL 33442-8190

Cover photo by Robert Duron, Santa Monica
Author photo by Paul Greco Photography, Manhattan
Special thanks to cover models Suzanne Whang, represented by Cunningham, Escott, DiPene,
    Los Angeles; and Dara Vin, represented by Halpin House West, Malibu
Costumes by Wendy Keller
Inside book design by Lawna Patterson Oldfield

"Do your relationships all seem like the plot of a horror movie? Wendy Keller has compiled all the information you need to get your life back on track."

—**Pam Lontos**
professional speaker and consultant

"This book is not just about a woman's sexuality, but her whole being. Wendy teaches you not to just become a Born-Again Virgin, but to become a Born-Again Person! Give this to every *single* woman you know."

—**Sylvia Green**
director, Malibu Matches

"*The Cult of the Born-Again Virgin* is outrageous yet true, sexy yet romantic. To her great credit, Wendy Keller writes about gender issues with wit but without the childish stereotypes that characterized the genre at the end of the twentieth century."

—**Gregory J. P. Godek**
author, *1,001 Ways to Be Romantic*

"Wendy Keller addresses our most complex subject with wit, skill and wisdom. This is THE single woman's handbook for the new millennium. It's a terrific and insightful read."

—**Ellae Elinwood**
author, *Timeless Face: Thirty Days to a Younger You*

"This book is to the women's movement what a college education is to high-school grads!"

—**Mark Victor Hansen**
coauthor, *Chicken Soup for the Soul* series

*Wendy Keller married at
nineteen and divorced at twenty-nine.
Since then, she has dated four zillion Mr. Wrongs
and asked five zillion relationship questions.
Wendy is a successful literary agent and author.
She lives in Malibu with her precious
seven-year-old daughter, Sophia, a dog,
two fish and a hamster.*

For Jeff Zhorne,
my ex-husband, who broke my heart,
and for others since who helped it stay broken
until I learned to heal myself.
Out of pain, I have grown.
Thank you.

Contents

Acknowledgments

To my precious daughter, Sophia Rose, thank you for being you! I love being your Mommy! If I had no reason to think of the example I am setting for you, I would never have chosen to write this book.

The women who planted the seed for this book are Iris Martin and through her Amy Karp and through her Allison Saget. Thanks, ladies! You've proven nothing is by chance. Thank you for your friendship, inspiration and fun-loving natures.

Humble reverence to the unseen hand that opened the doors for this book.

Since it is always done in book acknowledgments, I'd like to thank my marvelous, encouraging, stupendous agent, whose faith in this project never failed. Errr . . . that'd be me.

To my true friend Mark Victor Hansen, who believes I can do anything I set my mind to, that you can do anything you set your mind to and that he can do anything he sets his mind to (and he has certainly proven it). Thanks for lunch, pal. Your energy and faith always astound me.

Thank you to my parents, who teach me still about love.

My most sincere thanks and warm regards to all the women and men I interviewed, especially Betty. Your insights and candor will inspire the many thousands who read this book.

Thank you to Joel Millman, for teaching me how to write. To Fred Stewart and Don Sieh who wouldn't take anything less than my best.

Thank you to beloved friends in publishing who believed in me and always have: Rick Frishman, Leslie Meredith, Jennifer Enderlin, Pam Liflander, John Mahaney, John Kremer and so many others.

With profound respect and appreciation for my new friends: Kelly Maragni, Kim Weiss and Randee Feldman. If every marketing department had a team like yours, the publishing industry would be a lot happier and more profitable.

To my masterful manuscript editor, Heath Lynn Silberfeld, who brought insight from her knowledge in two important areas: the love of language and the language of love. Thank you for giving me the gift of clarity.

And finally, to my remarkable, clever, funny, charming editor Matthew Diener. Even though he's a *guy* he saw the promise in this title, unearthed it, and hopefully found another diamond for HCI and Peter Vegso's glittering crown of successful books. Gee, Matthew. Thanks a lot.

Introduction

It all began at a glitterati dinner party in the chic part of Philadelphia. A cluster of women, all wearing shapeless haute couture satin dresses our mothers would have worn as negligees, were sipping white wine and talking about *men* and *sex.* It was getting a little late. We were holding the last sparkling remnants of the party in our eyes.

Allison, who in real life is a nationally renowned special events marketing consultant, volunteered that it had been almost nine months since she'd had sex with anyone. The other women cried out with laughter and disbelief. "No, honest," she insisted, "I'm a born-again virgin!" We laughed at her clever joke, but in the weeks that followed, I heard women everywhere repeating the phrase. I heard it in a café in Manhattan, and I heard it again in the famous Polo Lounge in

Beverly Hills. "Born-again virgin." For me, it had been one husband, three kids and plenty of close male friends since I'd lost mine, and I wondered what these women meant. The idea intrigued me.

So I began asking. "Is it really possible to *reclaim* your virginity, that 'precious gift' your mom wanted you to save for your wedding night?" "Why?" "What does it mean to you?" "What could it mean to you?" "How could one accomplish this?" "Would being a virgin help you get a better guy—or keep the jerks and dolts away?" I asked women these questions, and I listened to their answers. As I asked, I found a surprisingly large number of single women who either were or had been what I call "born-again virgins" (BAVs). I heard fascinating stories from females just like you and me who got tired of wedding rings being hastily stuffed in trouser pockets and the meat markets and the singles scene and throwing on their wrinkled cocktail clothes and creeping out at dawn to wait by the phone for three weeks.

I heard women announcing their celibacy and/or their abstinence, or discussing the length of time they wait to "do it" with a new guy, how long they "check him out" first and what effect all this has on relationships. It was amazing. I had to learn more.

I heard stories from now-celibate women who at last gave up on him ever leaving his wife. I heard stories from other born-again virgins who gave up on him ever deciding what he really *does* want is a wife and kids. What I expected was bitterness and loneliness. What I found was power and joy, even financial success. It's compelling stuff.

These brave new women, these born-again virgin goddesses, are not a group of closet lesbians. They are not man-haters or ugly and fat and old. For the most part, the women I interviewed about their sexuality were under fifty, not more than ten pounds above "normal" weight (like most of us), as sensual and lusty as any of us, reasonably attractive, and mostly highly educated and particularly successful in their careers.

They decided to get off the hamster wheel of dating and sex and relationships and said, "I'm waiting for what I want, because I am worth waiting for." Curiously, in every single case, every woman who had chosen to find herself an interesting man *since* her personal declaration and return to virginhood believes she has attracted a "higher-quality man."

Finding a higher-quality man isn't the only reason women are choosing readmission to virginity. I learned that becoming a BAV isn't about "saving yourself" for some man who may or may not show up or who might appreciate you when he does. In many cases, women chose virginity to create peace in their lives, or to attain a higher level of self-actualization, or to achieve a sense of inner balance, to return to core values, or to explore more deeply their own spirituality. They did it to make more free time. Some wanted to make money by focusing on growing their business or career or to start a charity with their newfound strength and sense of purpose. One famous BAV did it to build a world empire! They all did it to get in touch with their creative selves, to gather up energy for a life transition, to heal from losses. There were all sorts of reasons and all sorts of benefits. It's fascinating stuff.

It didn't take more than a few of these conversations for me to decide to try it myself. I rationalized that it wasn't like I was vowing to enter a convent and there would be no going back, but I found when I chose *not* to focus on the fulfillment of my sexual urges, parts of myself I didn't even know I had flowered.

My relationships with all males deepened. When I decided to live my life without being wrapped around a penis, I found a whole transcendent sense of freedom and power, and I experienced true womanhood and victory far beyond my wildest fantasies.

In her book *Rich Is Better,* Tessa Albert Warschaw sums up the state of "manlessness" this way, reminding us, "We've bought into the myth that it's a Noah's Ark world, that an uncoupled woman is as useless as a leftover sock." If you think about it, there are many ways to form "people units" in our society. A male-female couple is only one of many. It's not the most common (mother-child is); it's not necessarily the most rewarding; it's not the only one capable of providing us with a fulfilling, interesting private life. But Warschaw is right about the way some women *feel* about being alone. Worse, the sense of feeling odd, lonely or left out when alone creates actual *guilt* in women who have been exposed to the prolific media on how "alone doesn't have to mean lonely."

The BAVs I interviewed had vibrant, multifaceted relationships with many people. These women weren't lonely. They weren't sitting home with a cat and a book on Friday nights, eating pints of ice cream—unless they wanted to. This was a surprising and critical discovery in the quest to understand the rising Cult of the Born-Again Virgin. But there are even more benefits!

> *Sometimes when I look at my children I say to myself, "Lillian, you should have stayed a virgin."*

> LILLIAN CARTER,
> MOTHER OF FORMER PRESIDENT JIMMY CARTER

In this age of STDs and AIDS and a society that places such a low value on commitment to marriage and monogamy, becoming a born-again virgin makes sense for a lot of women. It makes good sense to women who are just plain sick and tired of the games. It is the most logical choice for women who never really grieved their divorce or past relationship and who suspect that residual pain might be what drives their sexual and relationship choices now. For women who need to boost their self-esteem, becoming a BAV can be a critical key. It might be right for women who sense that something is missing and who don't think that missing piece is phallic.

Celibacy makes sense to women who are mature enough and ready to say "Sure, Prince Charming would be nice. But I'm going to live my life fully and live it for me and on my terms for now. And if he comes along, fine." And if he doesn't, well, that's fine, too. My observation is you've got a heck of a lot greater chance of finding Mr. Right when your raging hormones aren't encouraging you to say yes to any six-and-a-half-inch-long "prize" that's being offered.

In this book, you'll read about Allison, who sparked this idea at the cocktail party, and how amazing her life is now. You'll be introduced to a few of the thousands of women across this country who hear the rallying cry in their souls. I suspect you will be tempted by their power.

For those already committed to cherishing their hearts by cherishing their own bodies, this book will serve you like a chat with your best girlfriend and will validate that *you are not alone.* For women just beginning to explore the power of this option, this book will be your looking glass and you'll be Alice. In this book, you'll see how the choice to *make sex a choice again,* instead of the admission fee in dating relationships, empowers women to value their strength as women, their femininity, their contribution to a relationship, and their sense of self-worth and self-esteem.

You'll hear stories of how women sanctified themselves and set themselves aside for greater purposes in their lifetime. You'll meet women who without any religion at all found a resounding level of spiritual growth as a result of their decision. You'll be introduced to your long-lost girlfriends who found their men through the clarity of chastity and are living happily ever after to prove it.

In these pages, you'll meet women just like you who at one time thought the concept of voluntarily forfeiting sex was ludicrous but who later found it leads to amazing strength. Through the voices of your new friends, you will find answers to those questions that have been in the back of your mind for so long.

"Will guys still date me if I say no?"

"But I *love* sex! What about that?"

"Every guy I meet turns out to be a jerk! Where have all the nice guys gone?"

"But I'm in my sexual prime. I *have* to have it, don't I?"

"What do men think when a woman refuses?"

"Maybe I need some time off from dating. Will that be too weird?"

"How can I make him wait until I decide if I really want to get involved?"

"Isn't this an old-fashioned idea? Or some sort of religious thing?"

"Do I owe it to him? Does he think I do?"

"If I could just find more time in my life, I'd . . ."

"What if I'm the only woman in the world who wishes saying 'No, thanks' was easier?"

And many more. *Because this book isn't about not having sex.* It's about choosing if you will have sex, and with whom, and when. It's about a woman's right to choose—in more ways than one. It's about making the choice *not* to have it for a while (or a lifetime) perfectly cool.

In our headlong rush for independence, I suspect in some ways we've sold out as a gender. Like our mothers warned us, maybe men really don't go around buying cows when they are getting the milk for free. (Who wants to be a cow, anyway?)

While we all hold high the banner of feminism, as I know we must, somewhere in the frenzy of revolution some part of our souls has gotten trampled.

This book is about reclaiming your soul by reclaiming your body. Come visit with your sisters who are already members of the Cult of the Born-Again Virgin. You just might find you want to stay a while.

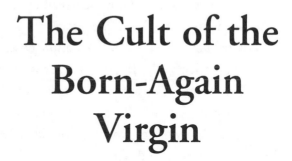

The Cult of the Born-Again Virgin

Some woman's huge breasts are about to pop right out of her pink sequined dress. I glance at her unnaturally perfect size Ds and those of the woman just a row away from her. She's a silicone job, too, and she has collagen in her puffy lips. Flawless. Amazing bodies, perfect clothes, makeup and hair. Where do they find these women? Are they perfect examples of what we all should be? I want to ask the guy behind me, who is also scanning the tabloid section.

Alongside these supermodels, the tabloid headlines very kindly offer to help me look just like these women, how to have an orgasm every time, how to determine if he's cheating on me, how to make sure I am giving good head and other important life skills. I look at the teen magazines. Yep, there they are teaching fourteen-year-old girls what to do with their fifteen-year-old boyfriends and with their zits.

An alien dropping in at the grocery store and scanning our tabloids would believe we are a nation obsessed with sex. Like Marlene Dietrich said, "In America sex is an obsession. In other parts of the world it's a fact." Having been to Europe, I'm not so sure it's just us, but we can all agree that sex is on our national minds a lot. We wonder what our president did with his intern. We wonder if that odd single guy next door is a pervert. We believe that *everybody* is doing it much of the time. Married people guess that at least all the *single* people are doing it like rabbits. Everybody else is having a lot of sex, most of it wild, exciting and kinky. You've seen *Baywatch*. You have the facts. I mean, if you're not "getting any," there's something wrong with you. Right?

Chances are you've been to the video store on a Friday or Saturday night. Chances are you've seen plenty of normal-looking people who were not wearing wedding rings checking out movies. Chances are plenty of those people won't be having sex tonight. (We won't even say anything about the married people not making love. If you've been married, you already know that part of the story.)

As a culture, we seem to assume collectively that everyone else is having a great life. Everyone else is out living it up, maybe even everyone except us. We feel pressure or perhaps a bit odd or a bit inadequate if we are single but we aren't out there "mingling." We should at least be running personal ads or something, shouldn't we? At least trying to get into a relationship or to get sex or to get something. We have to. We're liberated! It's natural. It's the human thing to do.

In modern America, women are taught in the media and the resulting environment that they love sex, that sex is good, that everybody is doing it, that they are weird if they aren't, too. We're encouraged to have a wide variety of sexual experiences. We're given volumes on how to please men sexually and how to have orgasms. A great deal of pressure is exerted on women to be available sexually. Women are ashamed to say no, afraid to alienate themselves from their friends, the male(s) in their lives or their society.

But a groundswell is happening on a national level, a groundswell of women who are every bit as interested in sex as the next girl but who are ready to take a stand, to stop the insanity of bed hopping or boyfriend chasing or husband hunting, who are ready to take a mature position in the matter and curb their hormones until and unless someone worth their precious time and energy comes along. These women have a new slogan: *Sex: It isn't just for playtime anymore.*

I call these women born-again virgins—women who have returned to the state of purity and control over their own bodies most of us knew as girls. These are women who are at choice now, no matter how rampant their sexual history. These are strong women who are "starting over" by cleaning their own slate, women who have said, "I don't like how this is going, and I am ready to take responsibility for my sexual habits, my health, my relationships and my life." Sure, it's possible. Honest! I did it myself.

The reality is we women are coming into our own. After toppling the towers of male power in the 1970s, women are waking up. We're realizing at last that the sexual freedom we have given ourselves since the 1960s might not be working for us anymore. It isn't getting us what we thought it would. We've had thirty years of it—a long enough test. It's time to think about a new approach—or at least to rethink our current approach. You are part of the movement of the future.

As participants in or offspring of the "Love Generation," we've finally realized that nobody was talking only about the sexual kind of love, anyway. We're ready for something more meaningful than complete freedom to screw whomever we want. We're ready to be the ones in control of who we are, what we do and how we use our bodies. We're ready for the courage to say no, just like long ago women considered it brazen or shameful to say yes. We're ready, at last, for the true fulfillment of the slogan "A Woman's Right to Choose"—to choose if, when, where and with whom to be sexual, without feeling sad, abandoned, dirty, guilty, neglected, tricked, cheap, lonely, empty or wrong, without feeling unfulfilled and maybe a teensy bit used. (Psst! Even though we rarely mention it, that is how most of us end up feeling about casual sex.)

Sex of itself isn't any of those negative things. It's the meaning we attach to it that gives it its power to influence how we feel about ourselves, our sexuality and the men with whom we have sex. We can choose how we want to live our sexual lives as single women, and that choice can begin at any moment. So how do we build that new relationship with our sexual selves? Read this book.

This book is *not* about not having sex. It's a compilation of thoughts, processes, ideas, methods, decisions, benefits, concepts and considerations shared by women who have made the choice to refrain from using their sexual nature for a period of time— or permanently.

It takes sex off one's activity list and puts it on the list of what is revered. It takes it from screwing somebody to making love. It takes it from trading off sex for affection, touching, cuddling, and hope and introduces holding out for sex that celebrates a truly loving relationship. It makes deciding to remain celibate and not to date a good choice, if that's what you want today, and for going back into the fray with your eyes open if that's what you want tomorrow. It's up to you to be conscious about what you do. The results will follow your actions, and yours alone.

Most people find they create relationships with people who are most like the parent with whom they have the most difficulty. Think about your own past. Isn't that true for you? Basically, if you wait to get to know a man before you get naked, you have the chance to choose something other than the same relationship you had with your parents. "Waiting to establish a real relationship before you become sexual with a man keeps women from slipping into the repetition compulsion," said Iris Martin, CEO, Institute for Corporate Therapy and author of *From Couch to Corporation*. "We unconsciously and automatically repeat our parental relationships in our psychological drive toward mastery," she explained. "You are doomed to repeat this negative process until you change how you act and feel." Becoming a BAV can be crucial to your healing.

Love, Sex and Trusting Your Heart

Jennifer met John at a quiet little hotel bar. He was charming, funny, and obviously bright and sophisticated. Their brief conversation ended when Jennifer's girlfriend walked in and the women left for dinner alone, but John had asked for her number.

The next morning, he called. "I don't know what it was about you. It was magical. I have to see you again before I go home," he said. He lived in faraway Chicago, but his company was thinking of starting an office in her hometown. He would be here to supervise it for at least two years. He seemed so worldly, so well mannered. She was excited.

She agreed to dinner that night. She even looked his company up on the Net and saw his name listed as vice president. Not being "easy" (her words), she went with no intention of sleeping with him. It just wasn't her style. They met at 6:00 P.M. She was playing it safe, and she picked *him* up at his hotel. He had his own table at one of the most exclusive restaurants in her city. The maitre d' greeted them personally. The service was amazing, the setting ideal, the food extraordinary. John was handsome, educated and articulate. He, too, was divorced—for four years now, he said, but what really touched Jennifer's heart was the conversation.

"It's like he was reading from my script when we talked. Everything was in sync—we had the same favorite books, the same favorite movies. He had the same spiritual viewpoint as I do. The same speakers and business leaders had influenced us. We loved the same activities and believed the same things about raising our children." Jennifer's head was spinning. Could it be true? Was this the perfect man for her at last?

Neither seemed to want the night to end. At 1:00 A.M., they closed down the coffeehouse where they'd been talking for hours like two excited children. John took her chin in his hands and lifted her mouth to his. He kissed her gently, softly, reverently. "I believe I've finally found my soul mate. You're the woman I've been waiting for," he told her. Tears in her eyes, she nodded. "Me, too."

They drove back to his hotel. Making love was suddenly a certainty. The sex was loving and beautiful. They explored one another's bodies as they had one another's minds. His plane left early, so she drove him to the airport the next morning.

He called that night from Phoenix. "I miss you already," he said. "I think I am falling in love." The words were music to her ears. Her own marriage had ended bitterly three years earlier. Single mother of two school-age kids, she was ready at last, and this was surely as close as she'd come to "The One."

John promised to call again the next day, but when he did, he sounded busy and distant. She understood—meetings, work, deadlines, little sleep. The next day, he didn't call as promised, and he had not given her the name of his hotel.

Nothing the next day either. Or the next. Or the next. Finally, a week had passed since she'd heard from him. She took the business card from her evening bag and called the number. The secretary answered. Is he in? Yes. Who is calling? She hung up.

Two hours later, she had a plan. It was a big risk, but she had to do it. She called again. In her best imitation southern accent, she called the secretary back. "This is Brenda from Mr. Thompson's office in Georgia. We're trying to send a Christmas gift to John and his wife, but Mr. Thompson doesn't have his wife's name on file. Could you please tell me what it is?"

Jennifer knew it was a long shot. She knew how she'd feel if the secretary had an answer, but she had to do it. Something was wrong with the way this romance was going. The secretary paused for just a second. "Certainly," she said. "It's Julia."

A knife ripped through Jennifer's heart. She hung up the phone and cried and cried. He called after that, once, from some other hotel, a month later. He was coming back to her town.

"Who's Julia?" she asked when she recognized his voice.

"What do you mean, darling?" he asked after a moment's hesitation.

"Julia is your wife!" she said.

"I have to go now," he said in defeat and hung up the phone. It was their last conversation.

Not everyone has a story as sad as Jennifer's. But the look of pain and sorrow on her face when she tells this story—now almost two years later—is enough to convince me that it still hurts. Jennifer says she never sleeps with anyone on a first date now—never, no matter how lovely or how perfect or how anything else it seems. When the conversation is close to great, she feels nervous. When the guy is handsome and "just her type," she feels uncomfortable, even wary. When the conversation is nowhere near as interesting or wonderful as she remembers it with John, or the man is unattractive or not physically interesting to her, at least she feels comfortable and safe. The result? She has dated guys who were "comfortable" and "safe"—which means she has dated guys she knew she didn't really like so she could be "dating" but remain uninvolved enough to prevent being hurt.

"Now I have a new lease on life," Jennifer says, changing her mood. "I feel positive and happy since I made the choice to not be sexual for a while. I know I'll go back to being sexual, but I am taking time to heal from what happened with John. I know it sounds dumb—the whole thing happened in just a weekend—but it really hurt me and opened my eyes to my own naive ways of thinking."

Music is playing in the background. The song offers suggestions imperative for Jennifer and so many women sifting through the wreckage of their past. The singer asks us to grieve all our losses one at a time. How many of your lost loves have been swept under the bed, forgotten but always present? Could the pain of the past be affecting your present choices?

Jennifer believes she'll know when she's ready to "get back in the water" and try dating again. She'll try trusting somebody again. I believe she's right.

Why Even Try?

Women like Jennifer, like me, and like the many women I interviewed for this book represent a portion of a wildfire national trend. More and more women each day are deciding to become "born-again virgins" (BAVs), whether they know to call themselves that or not. They are the women who have examined the alternatives and decided that having sex (including in some cases masturbation) is not helping them move toward their goals.

In her wonderful, thought-provoking book *A Return to Modesty*, twenty-something author Wendy Shalit explores the value of modesty in our culture and speaks of reason after reason why she feels young women in her age group are returning to "old-fashioned" values. Chief among them seems to be a sense of self-esteem and self-respect. Could it be that modest conduct creates a sense of self-respect?

This young woman didn't fight for women's rights any more than I did. I tell my forty-three-year-old girlfriend that I am writing this book and she says, "Oh no! No one who fought that battle wants to hear she was wrong! You'll get into trouble!" She fails to realize that without the women's movement, I wouldn't be writing this book—because the concept of choice still would not be in women's vocabularies. I owe as much to the movement and its leaders as every woman in America. I honor it by writing this, in the same way that subsequent amendments to the Constitution support the authority and value of that vital American document.

Changing the way we look at something is never bad. After all, if your current actions were enough to produce more of what you want, more of it would already be in your life. Do you have enough of what you want?

Why should we examine and perhaps change our way of relating sexually to men? I've discovered hundreds of reasons to refrain from sexual behavior for a while. The majority of people, however, apparently choose to refrain because they are looking for someone special and they want to remove themselves from the melee to concentrate on developing themselves and attracting the type of person with whom they really want to share love. Remember the old saying "You attract what you *are,* not what you *want.*" If we more fully develop ourselves—emotionally, mentally, physically, financially and in other ways—we will attract people to ourselves at our new, higher level.

Women have been socialized to believe saying no to sex will make other people, especially men, view them as bitchy or as prudes or weird or something equally distasteful. So we don't stand up for what we want—or don't want—sexually, or we just drift along, numb to our feelings but always somewhat dissatisfied. We give in to an avalanche of peer pressure. We say yes when we mean no, and we wake up feeling badly about it. When we pretend to be demure and weak and accepting about our sexuality, we attract people who will never really get along with us anyway. If we stand up for our rights and show strength, we behave in a confident, emotionally healthy way. Therefore, we attract confident, emotionally healthy people to us.

I've discovered born-again virgins are single and single-again women from all races and socioeconomic and educational groups. BAVs are women who are (or are considering) refraining from intercourse (or sometimes any manner of lovemaking) until they come to a place where they act totally out of conscious choice and are in control again of their sexuality. They are waiting until they can be confident enough in who they are to define what and who they want, or even if they want anyone at all. From that vantage, they can figure out how to get what they really, truly want.

Some women choose permanent abstinence. Some recognize that abstinence can prove a useful tool in the development of their higher spiritual nature or the achievement of their personal goals. Women choose to become BAVs for many reasons, each personally hers. These reasons include the following, in random order:

Personal Power

   To gain or enhance personal power

   To develop more physical, psychic or intellectual energy

   To expand your awareness

   To develop more of who you are

   To focus on your goals

Personal Growth

   To nurture yourself

   To restore a sense of dignity and elegance

   To breathe deeply and learn new ways of interacting

   To cultivate more power over your thoughts

   To stand up for yourself

   To think about what you really want

   To restore choice

To have time to sort things out

To prioritize your life more clearly

To set and achieve goals

To spend time in meditation in preparation for your next life step

To cultivate a sense of personal dignity

To enhance self-control

To enhance self-esteem

To accept your true power as a woman

To further develop a sense of power

To attain fulfillment

To reestablish your identity in the world

To change some aspect of your physical or emotional self *before entering a new relationship*

To break an addiction (love, sex, alcohol, drugs, *cigarettes*, food, *relationships*)

To finish college or get an advanced degree

To have more free time for hobbies or other pursuits

Relationships

To be peacefully single

To attract and marry the "right" man

To grieve lost loves

To heal from divorce

To repair a broken heart

To break the bonds of dependency on men

To develop relationships with women friends

To develop closer bonds with your child(ren)

To care for an aging parent

To get off the dating fast track

To prepare for your next relationship

To stop playing games

Sexuality

To regain control over your sexuality and sexual
expectations

To learn about your sexual needs

To explore a change in sexual orientation

To introspect your sexuality

To evaluate the role of sexuality when choosing a mate

To thoroughly evaluate a man before beginning a
relationship

Livelihood and Finances

To get finances in order

To make more money

To get out of debt

To set up your own household

To build your retirement fund

To build your assets

To learn to handle your money well

To focus on a career

To focus on growing a business

Spiritual

To change religions

To find religion

To find spirituality

To return to the religious values of your childhood

To return to a moral principle of your childhood

To open your awareness

To gain spiritual perspective

To comprehend inner peace

To create spiritual clarity

To move to a new spiritual level

To sanctify your body for greater service

To focus on God

To allow in Divine Love

To open the chakras

To set a moral example for your children

To serve your mission

To serve humanity

To learn to see with your third eye

To enhance meditation and focus

To open psychic channels

To marvel at Creation

To revere the Divine within you

To connect with Mother/Goddess

Physical

    To get in shape

    To compete athletically

    To change your appearance

    To have more energy

    To prevent disease

    To heal disease

    To learn wellness

    To learn to cherish your body

    To minimize the possibility of contracting a sexually-transmitted disease

    To deal with having contracted a sexually-transmitted disease

    To eliminate the risk of pregnancy

    To learn how your body works best sexually

    To change sexual preferences

    To integrate holistically

Let's think about this for a moment. If other women are getting these benefits out of changing their thinking about the way they behave sexually, isn't it worth considering? Could you be missing something after all? Is it possible? If you've read this far, sister, you may as well admit to yourself you're at least open to the idea.

What if there really is a way you can gain these things in your life? What if you could put yourself back into control of your own sexuality—instead of forking it over to a man, society's point of view or your girlfriends' ideas of what appropriate sexual behavior is for you? After all, who knows what really is right for you except you? Nobody.

Let me ask you a favor, please. Get out a pen and go back over the long list of potential benefits (and I'm sure there are more I didn't list) and check off the ones that appeal to you, the ones you can relate to wanting in your life, the ones that sound interesting. Then sit down, girlfriend, and make yourself a cup of tea. Grab a nice crisp apple and settle down to read this book. Because the things you checked off, somebody else already has. You want your share? Read on, honey, read on.

Why Ask Why?

He tricked me into marrying him. He told me he was pregnant.

CAROL LEIFER, COMEDIENNE

N o matter what your reason for picking up this book, in these pages you will learn how to clarify your goals about your sexuality and, from that, your life. You will learn how to manifest exactly what you want by controlling your sexual behavior or at least living more consciously in this vital area of life.

This book is for our generation. We are the women caught in the crossfire between our mothers, who had no choice but to marry for the sake of future economic and emotional security, and the high school girls we see selling out their souls and bodies and living lost in misery because they suppose they have no future.

We are the women who represent the first generation who has no actual *need* for men in our lives. We are confused and worried—what are they good for besides sex? We want to know. How important is being held and cuddled? The sexual explosion of the 1960s to 1980s has created thirty years of confused women. We don't know if sex is special and it's okay to "keep yourself to yourself" until you meet the "right" guy. We don't know if girls "just wanna have fun." We don't know what we, individually, think about our sexuality because we have endured an avalanche of information telling us "Of course you want this!"

It's hard to know what we really want and what we're merely supposed to want. Let's play out the scenarios in our minds. Do you secretly, in the privacy of your own mind, want to be with one wonderful loving man for a very long time? Or do you secretly want to be a hooker on Sunset and Vine, averaging five men an hour? Hmm. How about asking this: Do you want to keep living the way you've been living? Are you happy with your sex life at this instant?

Do you remember the feminist slogan, "A woman without a man is like a fish without a bicycle"? Do you secretly wonder if she's right? And if she is, what does that translate to in your daily life? What if she's wrong? What if fish simply *like* bike riding? Would fish rather Roller-blade?

Do we need men? It is my fervent desire to reopen this issue for every woman who reads this book. What is right sexual conduct for each of us as individuals? What will get us the results we want, once we figure out what they are? The point is *not* to provide you with the right answer from Mount Olympus or anywhere else. Sister, I'm still looking for it myself. That's why I did all this research, interviewed all these women and spent all these hours typing my results.

Am I a man-hater? Some will doubtless misinterpret my words here to suggest I am. Some will suggest I am trying to create a group of women who despise men and are not lesbians or nuns but still refrain from sex.

What I am is a respecter of my half of the species—the women. Long ago I went to a women's leadership seminar led by one of the most influential, powerful women I have ever met. We called this magnificent female guru "Queen Ernestine." Ernestine Fischer of PSI Seminars had fifty-seven women (no men) in that room with her. She asked us to stand up if we didn't like women—thought they were dumb, stupid, insipid or weak. I stood up, and so did fifty-three other women! (At the time, the three who stayed seated were wusses anyway in my view.) I learned to rethink my entire attitude on my gender at that seminar. I owe Ernestine a lot of thanks. I became glad to be a woman under her tutelage.

Examine your heart. Are you proud to be a woman? Do you honestly think most women are truly equal (or sometimes superior) to men? Are you impressed by the way most women you know handle their lives and relationships? I'm going to guess you're not. We need to begin treating ourselves the way we want to be treated. Others will follow suit. We need to find joy in our womanhood, instead of viewing ourselves as victims of oppression. If there's a glass ceiling in this building, let's build our own buildings. Becoming a BAV is one major way to do that. Our

femaleness is a strength when we use it. It is only because generations of women bought into the self-fulfilling "weaker sex" philosophy that we allow this silly behavior from women and
devalue ourselves as a result.

In Victorian England, sexuality was intensely repressed. Did
that make it go away? No. Rather, it increased the number of
whorehouses and neurotics. In our own time, women have been
intensely repressed. Does that mean we accepted our "second-
quality" label? No! Some have, and those poor dears act out the
role. The rest of us have become increasingly revolutionary.

One insipid or silly airhead may get the males of the species on
her side, but she alienates the other, wiser women and creates a
bad name for us all. She needs to be educated in women's power,
and we need to be conscious enough to welcome her when she
shows up and not allow men to judge our gender by her folly.

Strong women make the right decisions *for themselves* today.
For some, it means becoming a BAV, but your decision may
change tomorrow. One of the basic precepts of becoming a born-
again virgin is if you don't like what happened last night, you can
reenroll today. Your decisions may change, like most of our decisions do, many times over your lifetime. The right answer is *in
you* somewhere. The right answer is getting in touch with how
you really feel about your sexuality and celebrating your womanhood by honoring that part of you. It's a part of you that you
probably haven't thought much about since you lost your virginity in high school or college.

So many of us are sexual without giving it much thought. We
assume it's normal, that everyone else is doing it, that the guys
expect it on the second/fifth/first/twenty-fifth date. We forget to
check in with the most important person in this sexual equation—

ourselves. Yet we're the ones we always wake up with the morning after, no matter with whom we have slept. We divorce our feelings as easily as we divorce our boyfriends or first husbands—often with the same confusing and angry results.

> *You never really know a man until*
> *you have divorced him.*
>
> ZSA ZSA GABOR, HUNGARIAN-AMERICAN CELEBRITY

As Wendy Shalit says in *A Return to Modesty,* some women feel embarrassed that we wanted more from him. We feel bad we want him to call. Or like my friend Lori said, "I feel kind of special when a man opens a door for me. Is that dumb?" We are confused about men and our relationship to them, and becoming a BAV is a chance to sort all that out. If you didn't understand something at work, wouldn't you take time to ask questions?

What would change in your life if you decided to take some time to read this book and think through your sexuality—perhaps for the first time? Possibly, a whole new world could open for you! Possibly, you could achieve an ideal relationship—with yourself first, with others second.

This book is for single women who are not in a relationship or who are leaving the one they are in now. This book is for single-again women who got divorced and entered "crazy time," trying to prove they still had value on the market. It's for single-again women who left a relationship and checked into an emotional convent. It's for all of us who without much forethought decided to become frigid or promiscuous or to marry the first guy who came along because we were lonely, scared or running away.

You know what lonely means? The dictionary says, "Dejected by the awareness of being alone," which implies that *being* alone and *feeling* lonely are far apart. The latter is a feeling, the former a situation. Lonely is optional. We can control feelings by consciously focusing our thoughts elsewhere.

As for scared, I want to suggest we are *all* scared. We're scared to say no. In this age of disease and casual sex and lies, we're scared to say yes. After we've been burned a few times, we're scared to open our hearts. We're scared to trust—we've known too many scoundrels. We're scared to touch our inherent greatness—we've buried it so far down. We're scared to put ourselves first. We are the daughters of the 1950s, 1960s and 1970s, raised by good women who were themselves raised by women who believed a woman could not vote or wear pants in public.

We've come a long way, baby. Why doesn't it feel like it when we screw a guy all night and fit into size-five jeans and he still doesn't call the next day? Is it "all his fault," or are we failing to honor ourselves in our behavior? Are we living up to our greatness? What could our greatness create—in our own lives and in the world?

In his book *The Natural Superiority of Women,* author Ashley Montagu (honest, that's his name and his book's title) suggests that ancient societies based on a matriarchal model had less violence, more human rights, a lower incidence of crime per capita and more civilized characteristics. In short, it was a more peaceful, gentler world then. With the year 2000 here, we women know in our hearts that it's our turn again.

We hear the rallying cry and see women moving toward the presidency of our country. Regardless of what she attains in her lifetime, Elizabeth Dole surely has paved the way for our daughters. We envision women's rights having become a moot point in fifty years. We see equal pay as our due and greater pay perhaps not far off. We see rights, welfare and social services changing. We see ourselves at last as the competent, caring, dynamic beings that we are. We use our intuitive powers. We use our love to dissolve wars and violence and hatred. *Their way doesn't work*—and each one of us knows it.

Socrates wrote almost twenty-five hundred years ago that there is nothing inherent in a woman's nature to prevent her from "engaging in the social functions of the citizen," including "those of the Philosopher King, who is equipped to rule by virtue of wisdom." Socrates observed that this can never happen when women are mired in domestic chores. He theorized the solution would be the abolition of the nuclear family among certain groups and the promotion of society itself as the family in which divisive interests are eliminated. Of course, he was writing in a time when women were not even educated or involved in worldly affairs, but we still don't rule. It's been twenty-five hundred years. What benefits has society lost?

According to some scholars, the word "woman" originated to signify social status. "Wife-man" (or "wifman" in Old English) implied a woman was the possession of a man—her husband. It may also be concluded that she did not become a woman—or wifman—until she married. Therefore, before marriage one was a maid in one's father's household. What does "maid" mean today? It means a servant. A female went from being a maid to being a wifman. Hmmm. Sounds like slavery to me! Sometime around the fourteenth century, the "f" in wifman was dropped, which modified it into "wiman," and from there the step to "woman" was easy to accomplish. Makes you think, doesn't it? No wonder

there's a "battle" of the sexes! We, who have the ability to rule at
least equally, have instead allowed ourselves to be *possessions* until
very recently.

Friedrich Engels, that philosopher so influenced by Karl Marx,
wrote his 1884 work, *The Origins of the Family,* to explain his
anthropological viewpoint regarding how we might have moved
from a matriarchal society to our present patriarchal one. He pos-
tulates that there are three great movements in history: savagery—
marked by hunting and gathering; barbarism—animal-like
breeding and rudimentary agriculture; and civilization—marked
by art and industry. His purpose apparently was to discuss how
women's positions deteriorate outside communism.

In the stage of savagery, group marriage (unrestricted sexual
freedom) prevailed, thus paternity was impossible to determine.
Therefore, only the female line, or Mother Right, was recognized. The childbearing function, and thus the woman herself,
was held in high regard. In fact, in Engels' own words, "Among
the savages and barbarians of the lower and middle stages, sometimes even of the higher stage, women not only have freedom,
but are held in high esteem." This was true communism—
everyone contributed to the economy, no one was dependent on
another, and no distinction between the public and the personal
was made. Children were raised communally, and food killed or
found was shared. "Personal property" was not a concept, nor
was "my wife."

Woman typically had more respect and power at this time. In
Native American tribes, as in other cultures, it was not uncommon for an arranged marriage to take place during which the
marrying parties met one another for the first time. A young
brave came to live in the longhouse, run by women of his wife's

tribe, and he was expected to contribute to the family's food supply. If he did not, the female elders of the tribe could easily oust him. Women were the dominating power. They could dethrone a chief if they felt the need.

As the society became agricultural and the drive to hunt for food diminished, a division of labor became the norm. In barbaric society, men attended flocks and crops; women attended children and men. The paired family emerged, and to ensure paternity, women were held to a standard of strict fidelity. The notions of private property and paternity affected the overthrow of the Mother Right because women were rendered economically dependent on men to support and feed their children. The men wanted assurances that the children they were feeding and who would become their heirs were truly theirs.

With advanced civilization, the monogamy of the patriarchal family further solidified male supremacy. Engels suggests that this development fostered the first true class struggle—now woman was a second-class citizen and man was her ruler. Economic survival was at stake.

He writes, "Sexual love . . . had little to do with the origin of monogamy. . . . While in the previous form of the family [group marriage] the men were never embarrassed [lacking] for women, but rather had more than enough of them, women now became scarce and were sought after." In accord with this shift to patriarchal rule, women were then bartered and abducted, raped, and traded.

When the French social observer Alexis de Tocqueville visited the United States in the nineteenth century, he commented that the country's greatness was due to the equality of women and the fact that rape was punishable by death because women were respected and protected. Think about today: After an arduous court battle to prove it was really rape, or date rape, or some other form of rape, a man is likely to receive a mild punishment and walk away—and the woman is likely to be ridiculed for inciting the attack.

Engels believed communism would prevail on earth in due course. About the commencement of that "happy" event, he wrote, "What may we anticipate about the adjustment of sexual relations after the impending downfall of capitalist production is mainly of a negative nature and mostly confined to elements that will disappear. But what will be added? That will be decided only after a new generation comes to maturity: a race of men who never in their lives have had any occasion for buying with money or other economic means of power the surrender of a woman; a race of women who have never had any occasion for surrendering to a man for any reason but love, or for refusing to surrender to their lover from fear of economic consequences. Once such people are in the world, they will not give a moment's thought to what we today believe should be their course. They will follow their own practice and fashion their own public opinion about the individual practice of every person—only this and nothing more."

Is Fitting in B-a-a-a-a-a-d?

Like a flock of sheep in so many ways, we blindly follow what everyone else is doing instead of standing up for what's right. It's the herd instinct, which survives to this day. Sheep are easy to herd, because if you can get one or two of the leaders going in a certain direction, the rest follow blindly, even if they're all heading to the slaughterhouse to become lamb chops.

Our subjugation is the result of sheeplike passivity. Apparently, we have a cultural desire to do what everyone else is doing. Look at a group of high school kids. They all dress pretty much the same. They all want to fit in. Isn't it cute? Now look around your office. Look at what you and your best friend wore for a night on the town. Look at what you wore to the class you're taking. Dressing similarly implies a desire to fit in. This winter, most women in my age group, for instance, and in my industry, wore black or brown suits with white shirts. Mandatory with that was a pair of thick-heeled ankle-high leather boots. It was a uniform of sorts, as much as blue pinstripes used to be for male lawyers.

Is this the individuality we fought for? Have we grown, changed? Have we individuated? Or have we merely changed the pattern of the wallpaper on the cell walls of our stifled existence? Are we really happier? Let's figure this out together. When you dated a guy four or five times in the 1950s, maybe he'd marry you, so you kissed him goodnight. When you date a guy four or five times now and you don't have sex with him, he kisses you off. Today, conformity encourages sexual behavior as part of our lemminglike social structure, just as sexual reticence was appropriate in earlier times. We must stop being sheep.

Nonconformity, true independence, means *making your own choices*. It includes conscious choice about your sexuality—and from there, every other part of our lives. You don't "have to" or "not have to" have sex. You *do* have to be conscious about the choices you make in every area of your life, in particular sexuality. You must personally be aware of future consequences, both emotional and physical, and take responsibility for them. We each have the civic and personal responsibility to assert our independence in this arena as in any other. Simply because it's now "okay" or "cool" to do something does not mean that it's wise for you to do.

As our mothers used to say, "If the kid next door jumped off the bridge, would you do it, too?" If we've come so far, why aren't we living in Utopia?

In *A Return to Modesty,* Wendy Shalit states, "Now that we have wiped our society clean of all traces of patriarchal rule and codes of conduct, we are finding that the hatred of women may be all the more in evidence. But why, exactly? I think we might have forgotten an important idea, lost our respect for a specific virtue." She is referring to "modesty."

While some will dispute Shalit's assessment that we have "wiped clean all traces," we cannot deny that the fear factor for most women has increased dramatically. We now accept we must be afraid of rape, stalking, harassment, and in every other way used, manipulated, discarded, and unloved. We literally have created our own beds and now we lie in them. If this is equality and liberty, then perhaps we should find the middle ground, collectively and individually.

But it's not really us again them. We are co-conspirators, not victims. Men aren't the bad guys and we the sweet, innocent Sleeping Beauties lying around waiting to be kissed. We can change the social dynamic again if we revolt again, and we are! We are evolving into the new generation of Warrior Queens. Like Boudicea, the heroine of British legend, like Joan of Arc who led armies into battle for her noble cause, we are capable of anything upon which we set our minds. The question for each of us then becomes this: Upon what will we set our minds?

Women have the power to manifest change, and I suggest the

majority of our power comes from right in our wombs. We can use it to change the world if we will just learn how.

We've all had the experience of a man slobbering while trying to get us to say yes. We've all had some idiot wolf whistle as we walk down the street. So what does that prove? It proves we have the power they want. If we have the power to turn some of them into animals, it stands to reason that we have something they believe they want. We have the power to enforce responsible, healthy behavior.

Why do most newly divorced men remarry within eighteen months? And most newly divorced women wait an average of *seven years?* You guessed it! We're the ones with the power! In *Women Who May Never Marry,* social anthropologist Leanna Wolfe suggests that our real power is the ability to create intimacy with both genders. She writes, "The happiest females are often divorcees who have no interest in remarrying, while the most miserable males are recently divorced and not yet remarried." Why? Many women experience marriage as servants and caretakers to their husbands and children, and divorce often opens them up to a whole new world of freedom. *"Meanwhile, since most men don't develop ways to share emotionally as easily as women do, marriage remains the only arena many of them have for gaining the intimacy all humans need."* (Emphasis mine throughout.)

Craig, thirty-five, a gay male, told me, "My lesbian friends say foreplay takes four years. Two women focus on developing intimacy first, but some of the gay guys I know will do it with a stranger without words. Afterward they say 'bye' and go back to their friends and it's over. Men can displace their sexuality. It's the women who drive the desire for intimacy. Sure some guys want it, but overall guys aren't trained in how to get it."

Author and speaker Rod Kennedy has a Ph.D. in communications. He explained intimacy this way: "A lot of grown people are clueless about intimacy. We need to be talking to one another, sharing the details of our lives. Men aren't trained to communicate, because we're always on stage performing for the little girls and other boys. As adults, they read John Gray [*Men Are from Mars, Women Are from Venus*], which gives men an excuse not to communicate." Dr. Kennedy explained how he focuses on intimacy in his marriage, despite being on the road so often. "I'm on the road 150 nights a year, but when I talk to Janelle [his wife] on the phone, I feel her presence. I smile as we share all the little details of our day. I make sure I listen as well as share. It makes me feel like I'm home with her."

We're the ones who, while married, often say, "If he dies, I'll never marry again," and then once we divorce him (70 percent of divorces are initiated by women—and not usually because they have a younger blond male secretary at the office) we are the ones who know to take our time. We instinctively know that this is a very conscious, serious decision. We want to be whole with ourselves before we plunge back in, and clear about if we even want to.

It's true that I should never have married,
but I didn't want to live without a man.
Brought up to respect convention, love had to
end in marriage. I'm afraid it did.

BETTE DAVIS, ACTRESS

My first marriage was a form of indentured servitude akin to the way our mothers and grandmothers lived in the 1950s, except I was living it—voluntarily—in the 1980s to early 1990s. Ten years of this kind of marital "bliss" confirmed for me that I am not going to thrive in a marriage like that or accept those boundaries again.

I observed, in the last months of my marriage, that different women had created different types of marriages. Some had more equal relationships than others. A few seemed happy. Based on all my discussions and observations since divorcing, I see that almost everyone I interviewed for this book—married, divorced, never married, male or female—talks about "sacrifice" and "compromise," as if the very act of being in relationship implies modifying one's needs, desires and goals to cater to another.

If you enter into a contract, you want to be sure you know what you are compromising before you sign, and you want to know specifically which benefits you'll receive to make it worthwhile. How much more true this is when the compromises you will make affect *your entire destiny*. The question then becomes "Do you want to compromise? In what aspects of your life?"

How do you sort it all out for yourself? My way is not likely to be ideal for anyone but me, but I make my decisions consciously. I want to lead you through my words and the words of the women you will meet in the pages of this book so you can make your own conscious decisions about the way you use and value your sexuality and your essential womanhood. As we come to the time when women will reassume the mantle of leadership, we must each choose to live consciously in every area of our lives so we can become all we are capable of becoming.

I've chosen to interview lots of women about their sexuality. They come from all walks of life. They are divorced, divorcing, never married, angry with men, coquettes, therapists, speakers, doctors, mothers, teachers, single-agains, desperately seeking. They are you.

The ones I will hold up as examples for you to consider are those who have chosen to live consciously with their sexuality—whatever that means to them. They are women who honor their sexuality, who honor their womanhood. They are women, like you are becoming now, who are prepared to do what it takes to become the woman they have always dreamed of becoming.

> *I am becoming the man I always*
> *wanted to marry.*
>
> SOURCE UNKNOWN

As we women join together, we are building the community of thought in which our children will be nourished. We are raising the daughters and sons who, hopefully, will weigh out the issue of sexuality differently from how we did. They will begin the generations who accept fully the equality of the species, at the same time revering each sex's unique qualities and abilities. As with much else—beginning with providing the ovum that creates a life—the decision to create this vision for our children begins with a woman, with you.

As you read, think about your sexuality. Are you happy with the way you are living? Are you getting the results you want? Is the problem that there are no good men, or do you secretly suspect that you might not be ready for Mr. Right if he walked in right now? Do you lie in bed sometimes and want to cry because you are so frustrated with the type of men you seem to be attracting—and not attracting?

Are you like me? Are you like the rest of us? Do you sometimes think guys get all the lucky breaks? Do you sometimes wonder how supersuccessful women succeed? Do you sometimes think all you want is to wake up happy—in the right relationship with ideal fulfillment and the perfect guy beside you?

Guess what, sister? We all wonder these things at different times in our lives. We all wonder how to find the key to unlock the relationships of misfortune we are experiencing. Relationship books from tough-talking Dr. Laura Schlessinger to the soft-spoken John Gray make U.S. bookshelves sag. We read *The Rules,* and we break the rules. What we want is *Real Moments,* but does that approach help us get them? Where are the answers?

We wonder how in the heck we are supposed to prepare for Mr. Right. How will we catch him if we find him? How will we create lasting bliss once we do? Most of us have heard the metaphysical phrase "When the student is ready, the teacher will come." I suggest that applies to finding the good men, too. When you—you, yourself, your brain, heart, body, soul—are ready, the right man will show up, if that's what you really, truly want, but are you sure that's what you really want? How do you get ready inside your heart? Perhaps by becoming a BAV.

It's less about them than we think. I know beyond any shadow of doubt we attract what we are, not what we want. Am I saying that if we were married to some wife-abusing idiot alcoholic we are that also? Indeed not. However, I am saying that something in our psyches allowed us to so devalue ourselves that we were willing to stay and put up with the abuse the first time it happened and that something in your head is allowing him to mistreat you. *This book is about breaking that cycle so you stop attracting the wrong guys.* It's about honoring yourself literally and symbolically and thereby attracting others who will also value you at your new, higher level.

When I was married, my husband and I were in a car accident that left me scarred from my rib cage to my pubic bone and from my outer left knee to my left hip. The five feet of scars were ugly, red and inflamed for about two years. During that time, my husband literally added insult to injury by suggesting occasionally I was lucky he was married to me because it would be hard for me to find anyone new, disfigured as I was. I stayed—*and agreed with him!*

After I left him and prepared to make love for the first time in my life with someone other than him (yes, I was a virgin when I married), I cried as I told my new lover Roy about the scars. Roy lifted up my satin nightgown and kissed my scar, to my surprise and delight. I knew in that moment that my ex had been wrong—that it had been his own fears of me leaving and doing something with my life that kept him intent on keeping me from believing in myself. Something inside me had finally broken free. I had given myself permission to create a new life. And, sister, have I ever!

I have spent the five years since my divorce learning about myself, learning about who I am and growing into the woman I always hoped I would become. I figure I'll die short of the goal of perfection, but jeez, I'm having fun trying. I'm learning all sorts of things about women's power. As I observe the girlfriends who divorce and scurry into the first relationship that opens to them, or the ones who become militant feminist man-haters, I see that their choices all are truly about one thing—protecting themselves from pain and fear. Yet do such actions really deal with the fear that lives inside our brains? No.

Only we can do that, by entering the dark places of our hearts, affirming our womanhood and our power to choose how to use or not use our bodies as we see fit, based on a true connectedness with who we are and what we're worth and what we really want right now. By mastering the bodies we live in, we learn to master our lives.

The cult of the born-again virgins is about celebrating our womanhood. It's about finding joy in our minds, bodies, instincts, skills, goals and power as women. We are a bit more than half the human race. We all intuitively know we have at least as much ability at nearly everything men do. Our world barely depends on physical strength anymore, anyway. We are unique in so many ways. Let's celebrate and honor that uniqueness.

In *Love, Sexuality and Matriarchy*, Erich Fromm says, "There is little of a sex-specific nature left in the relationship between man and woman . . . [the] difference is shaped by matriarchal and patriarchal social structures as well as by the dominating orientation of the social charter at a given time." In other words, our abdication to second class is what created that opportunity for subjugation in the first place. We can choose a different option whenever it suits us to do so. Our pride depends on us choosing to do so.

So let's go, sister. Let's pick up our dignity, our goals and our dreams. Let's get ready to march forward—to get your life and mine and the girl next door's moving in the right direction. We can. We will. We are women—hear us roar!

THREE

Nowhere to Go but Up!

That girl is such a slut!
The only thing she won't go
down on is a Neiman
Marcus escalator!

EILEEN FINNEY,
COMEDIENNE

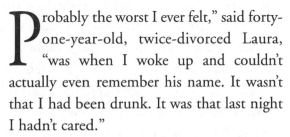

Probably the worst I ever felt," said forty-one-year-old, twice-divorced Laura, "was when I woke up and couldn't actually even remember his name. It wasn't that I had been drunk. It was that last night I hadn't cared."

Laura went on to describe the emotional pain that had led her to taking a stranger's

37

offer of a night's escape from her "real life." Her second husband
had been caught—in the arms of another man. It was more than
she could handle. Even though it had been almost a year, the
memory still haunted her. "Jim [her second husband] was so different from Ed [her first husband]. He was warm, patient, always
listened to me. He was never sexually demanding, always toler-
ant and kind," Laura said, picking at her nails. "I just couldn't
believe my eyes when I walked in that day. It was so horrible, and
he just looked at me. I think they were as surprised as I was."

Ghosts from our pasts can haunt our current sexual behavior.
Women who survived early childhood sexual abuse tend to treat
themselves with less dignity than women who did not endure
such trauma. Women whose marriages or relationships were
abusive and unhealthy can find themselves confused and afraid
when they leave. These experiences might make us feel out of
control of our bodies, less than who we are, small and weak and
vulnerable. Women from these situations sometimes immediately look for a man to "take care of them" or lash out with various forms of hostility against men.

Jill was repeatedly raped by an uncle from age eleven until she
was fourteen, when her mother remarried and they moved away.
Her being "safe" didn't last long, because soon her stepdad took
over where her uncle had left off. Jill told me she felt "dirty, useless, unloved and cheap"—and she lived out that belief about
herself. Many boys in her elementary and middle school classes
enjoyed their first sexual experience on top of Jill. By sixteen,
she'd had two abortions, one without a real doctor presiding.
The emotional and physical damage was devastating.

Somewhere in her early twenties, it slowly dawned on her that
she was now an adult and quite capable of choosing her sexual

partners. She began to develop pride in herself as something besides a sex object. She married a nice guy at twenty-six and has been married for fourteen years today. Jill reminds us, "The definition of insanity is doing the same thing over and over but expecting different results. I changed my behavior, so I got different results."

For some women, as for Jill, the experience of claiming one's own power is a slow dawning. For others, it arrives with a jolt of awareness, like it did for Laura. Either way, as exercise and diet maven Susan Powter says, it's time to "Stop the insanity!" It's time to claim who you are, to begin joyfully living your dreams for your own benefit. Now's the time, because there may be no tomorrow.

Most women do not have jolts of awareness. Rather, they know the slow burn of one failed relationship stacked upon another, upon another, upon another, until finally they reach the bottom emotionally. The pain becomes intense, and that's good because it makes us open to change. When we are at the bottom, we have to start liking ourselves again, even in tiny bits if that's all we can muster. Let's begin now.

Quick, grab a pencil. Nobody's looking. Now, in the privacy and intimacy you and I have created between the covers of this book, check off the traits you secretly like about yourself. Go ahead! I promise it will make you smile.

My Intelligence

I like the way I think.

I am logical.

I am always learning.

I get all the facts before I make a conclusion.

I organize thoughts, things and ideas clearly.

I am creative.

I respect intelligent people.

I have a degree in _____.

I learn fast.

I have good study skills.

I have a high I.Q.

I score well on tests.

Other: _____.

My Finances

I am wealthy enough to meet all my needs.

I am wealthy enough to provide some of my wants.

I live within a budget.

I don't live within a budget.

I am good at managing my finances.

I understand my financial software program.

I invest money.

I give money to charity.

I use money wisely.

I own a home.

I own my car.

I have no debt.

I have little debt.

I have debt because I invested in my education.

I have debt because I invested in my business.

I give good gifts to others.

I make great money.

I will make more money next year.

Money is not important to me.

Money is one of the most important things to me.

I am excellent at math.

I can always balance my checkbook exactly.

I am clever at being frugal.

I buy only quality items.

I live within my means.

I love to find good deals.

Other: _____.

My Body

I love my hair.

I love my eyes.

I love my skin.

I love my shape.

I love my low-cholesterol level.

I love my exercise program.

I love my commitment to my exercise program.

I stick to my diet.

I eat healthy foods.

I am a vegetarian.

I read about health and implement what I learn.

I am aware of my body.

I take care of my body.

I feel healthy.

I have great hygiene.

I take care of my teeth.

I am rarely sick.

I have a strong immune system.

I am pretty.

I like how I look naked.

I live in clean and tidy surroundings.

I am strong.

I am vibrant.

I enjoy physical activity.

Other: _____.

Spiritual Strengths

I believe in a Higher Power.

I live my life according to my ethics.

I have beliefs that support me.

I have friends who are like-minded.

I attend a congregation.

I find the spiritual in nature.

I meditate.

I pray.

I am psychic.

I am aware.

I am evolving.

I am an old soul.

I live my life consciously loving others.

I connect with my Higher Power regularly.

I am on a spiritual path.

I am becoming more enlightened.

There are teachers I respect.

I am conscious of my spiritual development.

Being a good person is important to me.

I believe that religion is for those who are afraid of hell, and spirituality is for those who have been there.

I do my best not to sin in accordance with the doctrines of my church.

A Higher Power is concerned with my well-being.

I take responsibility for my actions toward others.

I revere my body as the temple of my soul.

I honor others in my words and deeds.

Other: _____.

Good work! There are thousands more traits to like about you than I could possibly include here. You know what they are. Take a 3 x 5 card right now and write on it the twenty things you like most about yourself. Put this into your jewelry box because it's the most precious adornment you own. Read it aloud every time you open the box. Repeat it every day. Make another copy and keep it in your purse. Heck, repeat it a hundred times a day if you want really rapid results. It is all true, and you are as magnificent as you believe yourself to be. Others will only treat you as well as you treat yourself.

Millions of women can identify with the day their sexuality or dating life hit the wall, the day they began to "grow up," the day they said, "Okay, that's enough. I'm in charge here," the day they crawled out of a strange man's bed and slithered home and he *still* didn't call—or worse, she called him and his wife answered. From that point, there's nowhere to go but up.

For others, the bottom was finally realizing they were dying in their current relationship. Reaching bottom is characterized by depression, apathy, sadness, loss of sexual interest, overt sexual interest, a sense of feeling dissociated from your feelings, body, or other people, a sense of loss of happiness, or a feeling of despair.

Pain causes us to change, and change is good, but sometimes we evaluate the past irrationally and thereby reach irrational *conclusions.* We add up our experiences, look for patterns, and conclude "Oh! I shouldn't date men who wear khaki trousers" or an equally illogical *conclusion.* Smart conclusions help us. Erroneous ones keep us locked into bad habits. It doesn't have to be that way because, as Tony Robbins always says, "The past does not equal the future." You can make a new choice at any time. Remember, insanity is often defined as repeating the same actions over and over and continuing to hope for different results. Wise actions can be based only on logical "conclusions" and accurate information. BAVs make sure they get this information.

It's the good *logical conclusions* we seek, the true, honest ones based on who we really are and what we really think. These are the ones that will move us out of pain and into better results based on better choices tomorrow, and we get them by processing reliable data. Reliable data are the result of accurately and clearly inputting rational, empirical facts. How can you be rational about emotions? Through observation. Ask yourself the following (logical) questions:

1. Was your last relationship "successful" according to your goal(s)?
2. Do you feel positive or negative overall about your last few relationships?
3. Were there similar character traits in the last men with whom you've been in relationship?
4. Are any of these traits similar to the traits you saw in your parent(s)?
5. Are you *happy* with the results you're getting?
6. Did you act similarly in the beginning of each relationship? In the middle? At the end?
7. Are you open to changing yourself so you can change the way others relate to you?

The trick is to evaluate the data you currently have, find patterns and make adaptations as necessary. What results are you getting in your life right now? What actions are you taking consistently? What conclusions have you formed about your ration of success?

The good news is you can change your erroneous conclusions and behaviors whenever you want. The bad conclusions don't get you closer to what you want in your life. The good conclusions do. If you aren't tickled pink with your life right now, I guarantee you need to make some new conclusions and start living differently now.

Making a new choice is a good move. It can bring all the benefits we talked about in the previous chapters. Yet despite repeated bad results, one negative choice women seem to make for themselves repeatedly is in the area of sexuality. Perhaps nowhere else are we so influenced by the media, by what our high school girlfriends said or did all those years ago, by what we think other people are doing. How easy it is to lose touch with who we really are on this crucial subject, and how easy it is to get back on track. The first step is agreeing that your life isn't how you want it to be—and admitting, perhaps, that you've hit bottom, too.

As Ruth told me with a wink, "I'm a recovering tramp!" She laughed at the hyperbole and told me seriously, "These days, I don't get all crazed over a guy. I mean, why bother? I've evolved. Enough is enough already! I'm so focused on business now, I just don't have time for games."

I think the pain comes from our illusions about "how it should be." Weaned on the Sleeping Beauty and Cinderella myths we feed our children, we believe we'll be rescued or the Prince will show up someday and everything will turn out fine.

Women of previous generations married once, for the most part, and stuck it out no matter what. We bandy about the national divorce rate to show that people of a generation ago were happier in their marriages. I think not. I think they were just more committed to them, for whatever reason.

Today, when the pain is too intense, or when something more appealing comes along, or when rigor mortis begins to set in our hearts, we jump ship. We conclude that the current situation must be improved. We are left, or we leave. We hit the bottom of our tolerance for pain. However, the pain has caused movement, however long it took, and it is neither inherently good nor bad—it is simply a catalyst for movement or change, but you take one thing with you to the next relationship that will guarantee your repeated failure unless you take steps to change it. That something is *you*. It's your current beliefs that cause or prolong a false sense of low self-esteem. It's your own inability to live like the amazing, fabulous, dynamic, wonderful, precious woman you truly are. It's your inability to see her inside yourself and remind yourself that she is there. Open your eyes and look inside.

Foolish decisions lead to better decisions that lead to even better results in the future. Our mistakes are all so much water under the bridge, and just about as meaningful when you look back on your life at age eighty-five. There's nothing you can do to change it. You had to learn what you had to learn to be who and what you are today. Get over it and move on. Becoming a BAV is one way to do that. Reach new conclusions, take different actions and get better results!

Of course, after intense pain we can scurry to the opposite ditch and, rushing headlong into the arms of promiscuity, say "It doesn't matter how it turns out. All that matters is what feels good now." We can also say "All men are jerks" and not allow them even a chance. Modern women live on both sides of this road.

These examples of typical but illogical conclusions have far-reaching ramifications. In time, they will lead right back down into the depths of emotional despair where it's hard to see or be told that you are going in the wrong direction. Perspective gets murky the lower you go.

We make decisions every day. We make the best possible choices we can based on the information we have at the moment. We are all struggling to do our best and to create the best possible lives for ourselves. It's in our nature to do so, but sometimes we get ourselves into a behavioral rut. When we realize our efforts aren't working, it's time to change.

Change begins with the conscious realization that what you're doing isn't working anymore. Then, by seeing which beliefs led you to take your current actions, you can decide if the beliefs need to be changed. Probably one of the most common beliefs we hold in our innermost selves is "I need to be loved by someone else to prove that I am truly lovable." The unhealthy actions we take from that belief can make our whole lives a mess. We *must* invest in learning to love ourselves *first!* Take our your 3 x 5 card and remind yourself how lovable you are just by being you.

All humans want to be loved, cared for, nurtured and touched, especially those who did not receive adequate attention as children. At the very core of our existence, no matter how many layers of denial and resistance we have laid over it, each of us longs to be truly accepted and loved for who and what we are in the present moment. It's often more than we are capable of doing for ourselves. This is the very skill we must learn if we want to create wholesome relationships with men, our children, our parents and our friends.

The idea of becoming a BAV is less about learning to find someone who is willing to accept you, faults and all, as it is about learning to love yourself. When you love yourself and set your heart on treating yourself and others with dignity, you will naturally refuse to tolerate unpleasant behavior in others. You will demand respect—and you will find it. We all have had the experience of going out to the mall feeling absolutely on top of the world. In this state, people smiled at us, we found a great parking space and we found precisely what we were looking for that day. We also all have had the opposite experience of going out when we are feeling sick, tired or depressed and suddenly everything is a hassle. It works the same way with our interpersonal interactions.

One simple way to begin creating positive energy around yourself is by becoming "impeccable with your word." This means saying what you mean and meaning what you say. It means *never* criticizing yourself to yourself or anyone else and never gossiping. This principle is expanded upon in *The Four Agreements* by Don Miguel Ruiz. The beginning of creating honest, open, loving, trusting relationships in your life begins with controlling your tongue.

I dare you to try to say only nice things about yourself and others for seven days. The results can be profound. You may not only become more trustworthy, but also you may begin to perceive who you can truly trust. Trust is the building block of intimacy.

In our quest to find someone whom we can trust and who can trust us—someone with whom we can find and create a fulfilling, mutually nurturing relationship, we are faced with two options: Will we pile extra baggage onto our load by spinning through a series of unfortunate mishaps in our search for true love or will we protect our hearts and bodies as much as possible by honoring and nurturing ourselves unless and until someone truly interested in reciprocal loving comes along?

Those wonderful people are out there. They are looking for you as eagerly as you are looking for them. However, we build barriers as a society and as individuals. We say negative things to ourselves that create self-limiting beliefs. We say "I have to weigh just so many pounds to find the right man" or "I'm too young/old/ugly/pretty/smart/dumb to get into a real relationship" or "I never find nice guys." Tell you what: I have rarely met a man who wasn't either insecure about the possibility of losing his hair or his money or who didn't secretly worry about the size of his penis or his ability to use it well. Men can be every bit as neurotic as we are—but about different things. The bottom line is that the conclusions we make about ourselves and our lovability determine what we see when we look out into the world. By talking positively about ourselves, about the aspects of ourselves that we honestly like in this moment, we create a positive aura that is highly attractive.

In his unfathomably useful program "Personal Power" (the one advertised on the infomercial), Tony Robbins, the famous motivational coach, talks about the power of observation. In the words of the self-help gurus, "What you focus on becomes your reality." That is never truer than when it comes to our relationships. On his video and audio tapes, Robbins facilitates an exercise during which he tells listeners to look around the room and notice everything that is brown for the next thirty seconds, then to close their eyes and name everything that's green. The point of the exercise is that if we focus on the "brown" things in life, we will see only brown or, as my kid used to say, "poopy" things. If we focus on the great green living things, we will see more of those.

We have the power as BAVs to change what we focus on inside, deep inside where no one can see. We have the opportunity as BAVs to focus on personal growth—on changing anything we don't like about ourselves and on mentally and verbally encouraging what we *love* about ourselves. Saying nice things about yourself and others *to* yourself and others is like putting

Miracle-Gro on the flowers in your soul. From that vantage point, we create the emotional tranquility to reach new conclusions and develop better life skills.

As the Indian gurus have always told us, today we must fill out the shape of who we are now. Right now we need to become joyous and comfortable living in our bodies, minds and hearts. When we have achieved a state of peace with ourselves, we will have much more clarity about others. As such, we will set healthier standards when it comes to allowing others into our lives. We will make strong, healthy conclusions about who we are and with whom we want to spend time.

In the Center

We so often live our lives feeling off balance and uncentered. There are so many days when we feel like we just cannot catch up, cannot get a handle on how fast everything is going. Do you ever wish you could create a little space for yourself—take a couple of days off to just relax and be you without having to use sick days? We all sometimes think about how nice it would be to have someone take care of us, to have summer vacation again like kids do. We all want to have someone else cook dinner sometimes and to relax and just play. Many of us have not created lives that allow us much space to relax. Whether you are a single mother raising two kids or a CEO managing two hundred people or somewhere in between, time for yourself is sure to be a scarcity.

One reason we don't have space for ourselves physically is because we don't have space for ourselves mentally. I can remember my mother yelling at me and my two brothers, "Will you kids calm down? I can't even hear myself think!" That meant she was close to snapping, so we would certainly calm down lest we got in even more trouble.

Where do we find space to think? We find it by creating peace in our external world even for a moment. This is done through prayer, meditation or simply quiet introspection. Some people find the space through journaling. Some people say, "Oh, I don't have time to meditate or to think!" This is a catch-22 situation: Unless you take the time, you won't have the time.

If you will just take a few minutes when you first wake up and right before you go to bed to do the following exercise, you will begin to transform the quality of your real life—your inner life.

Here's the exercise:

Get comfy and take deep breaths three times, in through your nose and out through your mouth. As you exhale, say "Three" in your mind. Take two more breaths, and say "Two" each time in your mind as you exhale. Finally, take one breath and say "One" as you exhale. Next, in the silence of your mind, announce ten things you're grateful for and ten personal traits off your index card you're grateful for, too. By name, send love and healing energy to five people you know who need it. Still breathing deeply, repeat to yourself, "I love and respect myself and others. I honor myself and others with my words and actions. Others honor and respect and love me." Picture yourself walking peacefully through your favorite place in nature, happy and fulfilled. When you are ready, open your eyes.

Some research indicates that the human brain has more than 400,000 thoughts during the daylight hours alone. From "The alarm is ringing" to "Where did I put that customer's phone number?" our brains are crammed with all sorts of thoughts all day. Plenty are subconscious, but there are lots of conscious ones, too. What we will wear and what we will eat are usually fairly conscious thoughts.

You've heard that our brains are sixty zillion times more efficient than the best computer-operating system Bill Gates will ever dream up. Since we really do have all these thoughts and more daily, doesn't it make sense that if we harness a fraction of them we can create a totally different kind of life?

If the majority of our 400,000 thoughts are focused on fulfilling endless needs, it makes sense that we live our lives while treading water. The only true growth can come from stepping back, observing the whole, and determining which actions are bringing us closer to true fulfillment of our true needs and which are moving us or keeping us further away. Being a BAV will help you sift through your life and see what's working and what isn't.

The brain is the physical organ that is run by some unquantifiable essence called the "mind" or the "soul." Your mind/soul is the thing that drives the body in which you live. It's the only thing no one else can make you use, and it's also the only thing only you can put to good use. In *Man's Search for Meaning,* Viktor Frankl speaks of his life in Nazi prison camps. He writes that the survivors were the people who had something to live for when they got out. The survivors focused daily on the life they would have afterward. The mind is the only thing that could not be controlled, even by the prison guards. It was the one thing that determined one's chance at life on the other side of the prison-camp walls. The fact is you control your brain—it doesn't control you. Use that knowledge and master your world.

If you were going to change the way you live, change the pace of your life, stop having so much stress and such a hectic existence, you'd have to gain control over your mind, wouldn't you? You'd have to make new choices as a result of your new conclusions. The meditation exercise offered previously is a great way to begin.

The choices we make with our minds are driven by a number of factors, based on what we need. Psychologist Abraham Maslow addressed what motivates us in his "Hierarchy of Needs," a scale he created to delineate what drives people's behavior. Ideally, we move from the bottom to the top of his hierarchy (see chart below).

Some professionals suggest that people whose lower needs are not met or are thwarted for long periods of time can develop a permanent need that cannot be satisfied. (This is exemplified by people who lived through the Depression and still hoard string and newspaper to fend off scarcity.) Some people experienced a glut of something as kids, and they seem to go the other way, depending on whether or not they liked the excess. They either try to recreate the comfort of the glut or they completely avoid it. (Think about men you've met who want to marry their mothers and recreate the glut of maternal affection.)

Maslow's Hierarchy of Needs

- Self-actualization—A Life of Fulfillment
- Need to Feel Worthy
- Need to Love and Be Loved—Belongingness, Community and Family
- Need to Feel Safe and Secure
- Need for Food, Water and Shelter

ABRAHAM H. MASLOW—*TOWARD A PSYCHOLOGY OF BEING*

The bottom rung of Maslow's hierarchy is basically about staying alive. What drives people at this level is getting enough food and shelter for themselves and their families. Most people reading this book will pretty much have a dry roof over their heads and have eaten at least one meal today.

The next level is about safety, the need to feel like your life and property are secure. People who did not experience personal safety as a kid, especially, spend a lot of their adult lives trying to attain safety. They are trying to avoid bad, dangerous people in their lives and trying to get out of scary situations. We all need and require safety to function. That's why a near-miss in your car rattles your nerves at such a deep level: It affects your safety.

Next, Maslow says we want belongingness and family, to love and be loved. Belongingness is a sense of having people who care about you and whom you love. This includes your family, your kids, your colleagues, your friends or a mate. Again, people who were not connected or who were too intensely connected as kids will grow up seeking to compensate for belongingness in their adult lives, depending how they think about the belongingness they experienced as kids.

Next comes worthiness, which is feeling like what you are doing is of value. Last in the hierarchy is self-actualization.

Have you noticed where you probably are right now on Maslow's hierarchy? Where you are determines two things: what's most important to you now and the next milestone on your path of personal development. Both of these are helpful to know.

Further, it appears to me, although I am not a psychiatrist or a social scientist, that people seem to need the three lower-level commodities in different amounts. Once we get a house, we don't have to worry about that dry roof, so many of us begin looking for the next, bigger house. Once we get to a subsistence or acceptable level in each area, we backtrack, trying to bolster what we have in each category of need. Either we move on or we spend time fussing over things that are handled but not ideally handled. An example of this is thinking "I have a car, but next year I want a new car. The year after that, I want a sports car," and so on while never being grateful and peaceful about what we do have.

Another example of this that I have observed is that if you grew up in poverty, once you figure out how to make money, you are likely to pursue that with a vengeance induced by the lack of it in your childhood. Rather than money being about providing a nice standard of living, money becomes its own object or goal, relentlessly pulling harder.

Also, if you grew up with a large family of cousins and aunts and uncles, and you loved it, you're more likely to be looking for a wide social network as an adult, and you will get involved more eagerly with things that support your sense of belongingness. On the other hand, if you hated it, you're likely to not have children and to be pretty low-key in your social life. These are conclusions reached by erroneous data you absorbed when you were immature and may have nothing to do with what you'd really like today.

I am theorizing that we try to compensate for extreme lack or extreme abundance when we become adults or that we try to re-create our childhoods as closely as possible because that makes us feel comfortable. It depends on how we *thought about it* when we were kids.

As we move up the scale of needs and arrive at belongingness and love, we look around and see the nuclear family as the accepted social unit. It is our current conditioning to believe that the family is a husband and wife, two kids and a dog in a house with a picket fence.

Before the Industrial Age, the family was everyone you were related to by blood. They typically all lived on or near the same farm and spent their entire lives working, eating, sleeping and playing together. Then primogeniture—the inheritance of the parents' wealth by only the firstborn male—kicked in, and thus began the reality we have today. Since people had plenty of kids so they could have free help on the farm, a lot of people were displaced once Ma and Pa kicked off and big brother inherited everything.

The Industrial Age filled the void by creating the promise of money and excitement in the big city. While the reality was more often poverty and sweatshops, the cities provided a haven for people starting new lives. This meant they were away from their families for the first time and perhaps for forever. Add to that massive immigration and the beginning of America's population growth, and you see more and more people were looking for work to provide food, clothing, and shelter so they could build safe homes and find a great sense of community and belongingness. That last need is why in certain parts of big cities—for example, Los Angeles, New York and Chicago—there are to this day communities where you can live your whole life and die without ever having had to learn English.

When people are forced to move into a new environment physically, they simultaneously are forced to change and adapt and grow emotionally. Humans tend to resist change because it requires modifying oneself on so many levels. In the instance of people leaving the farm for the city, so much movement away from the nuclear family forced people to grow emotionally.

People formed new communities with strangers. Women pretty much had to marry. They would have been a threat to these new, loosely held together communities if they didn't because of the need for the higher wages paid to males for survival and because the sex trade was one of the only avenues left for women to earn living wages in this polyglot. Stable women married, reproduced and helped stabilize society. That's pretty much how it was until World War II, when women suddenly were called out of their increasingly comfy domestic lives and into filling vacancies left by men who went to war. Left alone, women banded together and formed their own communities and their own sense of belongingness, which has never been broken since.

When the men returned from the war, the U.S. government offered all sorts of incentives to women to give up their jobs and go have babies in nice little government-subsidized tract homes. So they did. They physically moved from the workplace back to their homes—and stayed there until they got bored with belongingness and community and moved on to the next level: the need to feel worthy or to have a meaningful life. Enter the feminist revolution! Viktor Frankl wrote *Man's Search for Meaning*. Betty Friedan wrote *The Feminine Mystique,* which could be loosely retitled "Woman's Search for Meaning."

Now women had to have meaning in their lives, a sense of feeling worthy. So, like gum stuck to the bottom of a shoe, we yanked ourselves off the boring linoleum of rank-and-file domesticity and took off at a run. Some of the gum still remains, though. It is evidenced in our lingering belief that our belongingness needs cannot be met without a family of one sort or another and the picket fence erected around us. That conclusion is based on erroneous data.

"Family," as we have just seen, has meant various things at different times in history. What it means today is not likely to be what it means in fifty years. The essence of family, the cement that brings and holds people together, is the need for belongingness.

History has shown that there are certainly other ways to achieve a sense of belongingness, other ways to create families. At this time in our evolution, we can choose to create a sense of belongingness in our workplace, at school, in our community, at church, in the arts, with friends or with our special interests. The need for belongingness can be met in a variety of ways, and, in fact, it is currently considered unhealthy to expect to fulfill your entire need to belong from one individual or group. We label what was normal fifty years ago as "codependence" now. Today's forward-thinking BAVs move physically (out of strangers' beds) to catapult themselves emotionally onto the frontier of self-actualization, but we all retain the basic human need for belongingness.

However, you cannot see your need for belongingness when you are right in the middle of it. It's just like a bum scrounging for food. He doesn't think "Gee, if I eat this stuff I just found in the trash, I could get really sick from the germs." He thinks "Feed me! I'm starving!" He has a need, and he wants it filled. Typically, he doesn't take the job placement training offered at the shelter. He doesn't take the steps required to (re)build a life that would truly satisfy the need for food, clothing and shelter.

We've created microcosms for ourselves in our society. In our Internet world of dissociations, we send emails to our mothers to keep in touch. We forward jokes to our "best friends" on our mailing list to let them know they are on our minds. We have created a society of emotional hermits—in part due to a tsunami of burnout we feel in response to the rift generated in the foundation of our sexual behavior during the sexual revolution of the past thirty years. We've lost our sense of community, of belongingness. Like the bum seeking food, when we are in the place where we crave belongingness in our hermetically sealed lives, we cannot pan out and view the situation easily. We cannot evaluate all the ramifications of each choice. We limit our ability to reach good conclusions because we allow in only limited or faulty data. We simply say, "Get me a man! Get me sex now! I'm starving to belong to someone or something! I'll take what I can get." However, once again like the desperate bum, we have better options we aren't taking.

Billions of dollars are funneled into the social services every year. Billions. If the bum really, really, really wanted a place to sleep, a shower, and a warm meal, not only could he go to a shelter, but he also could choose to get free training in job skills, break the cycle of drugs or alcohol (if applicable), and find work. We sometimes delude ourselves that all these people used to be CEOs of Fortune 500 companies who were broadsided by circumstances and are now homeless. The reality is far different. The bum could choose a different life if he wanted. At any moment, he could decide his life isn't working for him and move physically to create emotional changes in his life.

If this is not the politically correct viewpoint, tough. I have firsthand experience dealing with street people, and I can assure you plenty of them are not mentally capable of making new choices due to malnutrition or depravity and the like, but they were once when they had the chance and they didn't take it. (FYI, I'm not against helping people. In fact, I am a regular contributor to Habitat for Humanity, because I see that this organization helps people who really need help—and who help themselves—to get back on their feet.) The bum could have taken a chance when it was offered because opportunity, despite the adage, knocks often, just in different guises.

How does this directly apply to you? By considering becoming a BAV, you are being given a chance. You have the opportunity to change the way you fill your need for belonging, which will liberate you to fully explore higher levels of worthiness and self-actualization. You are being encouraged to find other ways—and there are many—to feel part of a community. You are being encouraged to make your life work for you right here, right now, with or without a man, through giving yourself a sense of worthiness and moving toward self-actualization. You are being given the precise method to pull back from your current life, examine your behavior and the results you are creating, and make different choices.

If the bum once had a glimmer of what was possible, but stuck another needle in his arm anyway, he was making a choice. His current reality is the result of lousy choices. If you feel totally depressed every time you really, really fall for a guy and he moves on, duh: Make different choices. If you feel anything negative at all when you wake up the next morning after screwing somebody you don't love (yet), make different choices.

If you don't like how your life is working, change it. It's pretty much as easy as that. You think all that advice to "just change it" is feel-good self-help bull-poopies? You think I don't know what it's like to deal with real problems like yours, that I don't have a clue how to make real choices, despite real pain, and to live happily again? Guess again, sister!

Remember the accident I told you about earlier and the five feet of scars I got? What I didn't tell you is how it happened, but now I will.

In March of 1991 my husband and I took our children to England, partly for holiday, partly for business. It was to be a much-needed chance to spend extra time with them.

After fifteen hours of plane time from Los Angeles, we finally arrived. We rented a car so we could tour the Cotswolds, the part of England with all the charming thatched cottages. Our second evening there, it began to drizzle. The children were napping in the back seat. Amelia rested her head on the side of her car seat—she'd just turned eighteen months old. Her brother Jeremy, age four, woke briefly to complain that he was hungry and fell back asleep. The jet lag was hitting us all.

We pulled up at a rural intersection and began driving through. Suddenly, a car hit us at seventy miles per hour! I took all the impact in my passenger door, and the car hurtled around and into a ditch. I looked down at my leg. My hip was where it always was, but my leg was wrapped around the imploded door like a piece of Silly Putty. The seatbelt had been thrust up under my rib cage and was crushing my lungs. My body was wickedly pinned to the drive shaft, and I couldn't move my head.

Like any mother, my main concern was for my children. I began calling out their names, screaming them, really. I had to know what had happened! My husband was mostly uninjured and in extreme shock. The driver's seat was relatively untouched, so he was able to get out. People began to gather. I screamed for my babies. There was no answer.

My daughter was dead and my son never recovered from his severe brain damage. He died three days later. I was extracted from the car hours after impact because I had almost become a part of the car, and they had to cut off the roof to get me out. I had broken everything on my left side from my knee to my shoulder and suffered severe internal damage.

The prognosis was bleak during my months in hospital. Bits and pieces pasted together amounted to me guessing that I would never have a day I didn't think about my children without pain. I would probably never walk normally again or ever bear another child, or have a happy day again in my life, or a day without physical pain. Even my marriage probably would not survive.

Sitting in a wheelchair in front of two coffins was the hardest experience of my life. I had nowhere to go but up if I was going to stay alive.

The specialists were wrong about everything except the last forecast. I divorced in 1994, but not before my husband and I had one more child together. Sophia is seven now. I own a thriving business. I live pain free. Most people perceive me as happy and bubbly and are surprised if they find out about the accident because my personality doesn't match the trauma I've endured. I can honestly say that my life is a dozen times better than it was before they died. *I made it that way. I made choices. So can you.*

Through Tony Robbins, Brian Tracy, the late Tom Wilhite, the influence of Char Margolis, and other living, dead and eternal teachers, I made it past the worst crisis of my life. Am I superhuman? No way! I simply made conscious decisions each day to change my life for the better. What place does this have in a book about born-again virgins? A *big* one. I add it because I want you to know I'm as normal as you are. I know life sucks sometimes. I'm not gifted or special or superhuman because I survived this tragedy. I am living proof that common people can survive and thrive again after uncommonly awful experiences. If I can survive and change a really bad life into a pretty fantastic one, so can you. Trust me, dear friend. You're in charge of the quality of your emotional life. It all begins with the decision to make it better, and then following through on that decision a little bit every day of your life. It's a cumulative thing. You can do it. Really, you can!

Abraham Maslow was intrigued by his studies of people on the path to self-actualization, the highest need on the chart he created. In 1970, he wrote a book called *Motivation and Personality,* in which he discusses persons who are above average in their ascendancy toward self-actualization (which again is living more of one's full potential). He talks about the sex drives of such persons, observing, "Self-actualizing men and women tend on the whole not to seek sex for its own sake." He states that for self-actualizing people, they tend to see sex as a "profound" and "mystical" experience, but at the same time, while they appreciate it more, he found they are also better able to handle the absence of sex in their lives. In summary, he found they have better sex and are in touch with their sexuality in general and its ramifications.

Isn't this interesting research? Because if Maslow is correct, then perhaps the opposite is true also. Perhaps self-control, discipline and dedication can accelerate the process of self-actualization to honor the self that is inherent in the decision to refrain from spurious sexuality. The born-again virgins of this and preceding generations were onto something. Maslow also found that "Self-actualizing people don't *need* each other as do 'ordinary' people. . . . Throughout intense [relationships], they remain themselves and remain ultimately masters of themselves as well, living by their own standards even though enjoying one another intensely." You have to reach at least a temporary plateau of maturity to give yourself a fighting chance of finding, attracting and receiving the right men and women into your life.

Self-actualized people are far removed from the shackles of codependent, jealous behavior. They allow others room to grow *not* by consciously allowing freedom but by the very nature of their own independence and growth. This possibility surely encourages all of us to work to move up the ladder of Maslow's Hierarchy of Needs to achieve maximum personal fulfillment.

Remember, when you move your body physically, you force yourself to grow emotionally. Make better choices to get better results! I *know* you can. I *pray* you will.

FOUR

Do Men Appear on a Woman's Hierarchy of Needs?

I refuse to consign the whole male sex to the nursery. I insist on believing some men are my equals.

BRIGID BROPHY, ENGLISH WRITER

L et me tell you a story of a woman who needed a man in her life, or so she thought. This is the story of Marie— the only thing I changed is her name. She was mentally in fantasyland when I met her. All through college, Marie wanted to get married. She had already handmade her own wedding dress and, in magpie fashion, wedged into storage at her mom's all the dishes, china, pots and pans that any woman would need in a lifetime. She had been waiting for her moment of glory for years. She had the wedding all planned in her mind. She even showed me a guest list. All that remained was to find a willing groom. She knew her life would begin as soon as she secured him.

Marie, like my second-grade daughter and her friends who play "bride" at dress-up, was caught up in the fantasy of her imagined wedding day, of being the center of attention for twenty-four hours, of being somebody, in this case, "Mrs. Somebody." Her focus was on that event because, at twenty-three, she believed it would give meaning to her life. She had reached the dangerous conclusion that a man would solve her problems and usher in a life of bliss. She could begin fully living her life then. She would tell me she just "needed to find the right guy." Eventually, she found a man who thought it was great that she was so prepared for matrimony. They married in haste and repented in leisure about five years later.

For some reason, Marie formed the conclusion that someone else was responsible for her happiness, her livelihood and her support. She had decided she needed help, that she should put off her life so she could more capably accommodate someone else's desires, the desires of someone she hadn't even met yet. The truth is that women are not fragile, helpless creatures, and we don't *need* men. We've proven *that* beyond all shadow of a doubt. We've taken over large parts of this culture. We support ourselves. We educate ourselves. We might not be at the very top of the socioeconomic food chain, but we're getting closer every day.

Are Men the Problem?

In his book *The Natural Superiority of Women,* Ashley Montagu states, "When men understand that the best way to solve their own problems is to help women solve those which men have created for women, they will have taken on the first significant steps toward its solution. And what is woman's greatest problem? Man. For man has created and maintained her principal difficulties, and until man solves his own difficulties, there can be no wholly satisfactory solution of woman's."

If men can run the world,
why can't they stop wearing neckties?
How intelligent is it to start the day by tying
a little noose around your neck?

Linda Ellerbee, writer, TV journalist,
documentary producer

It seems at first glance that we've come a long way since Ashley Montagu spoke out for the opposite gender, but have we really come that far or have we merely gained power then found ourselves overwhelmed with the dual responsibilities of home and career even if, as we now know, there is less inequality in the workplace? In Montagu's day, women could earn their livings in only a few ways, despite the fact that during World War II they had proven their competence at all sorts of jobs. Still, if she was unfortunate enough not to find a husband right out of high school, a young woman in the late 1940s or 1950s could take a job as a secretary, a factory worker or a teacher, or in some other acceptable "feminine" pursuit. Only these vocations were considered seemly for a woman. Talk about career options! Was this suppression or freedom?

Yesterday, I drove down the hill from my house toward the beach. On the way, a team of workers was repairing a phone line. One of the workers was a hefty woman with short curly blond hair sticking out from under her hard hat. She was single-handedly yanking a heavy tool of some sort from the back of a truck. Three men were watching her. I have to ask you, is that progress? Is that what we wanted when we claimed equal rights? Isn't it true that if she were a man, she could have asked for help without being accused of being weak or that one of the guys might have offered her a hand on his own?

I wonder what her life is like. She is still on the frontier of the women's movement. I wonder what made her choose that line of work. Surely, she is psychologically in the line of fire every day, as men decide to feel threatened and lash out at her or make her job more difficult.

Not long ago a man would offer a woman his seat on a public conveyance if she boarded and there were no vacant seats. Now we're more likely to have to compete with a man for that same seat, and tough luck to the little old lady left standing in the aisle.

Am I suggesting we go back to such forms of social courtesy? Am I blind to the fact that this "courtesy" represented the viewpoint that we were weaker and needed to be cared for by the stronger, wiser sex? I don't know about you, but if a guy opens a door for me on a date, I sometimes get confused. Maybe I should be insulted that he thinks I am so helpless. Other times I rush to open the next door so that he knows I am a full-fledged woman of the new millennium. Sometimes I think, "Aw, how sweet!" I'm confused! What about you?

According to the women I have spoken with, their attitudes shift from situation to situation. In contrast, have you ever watched a group of businessmen coming back from a luncheon? The first one to the door opens it and the rest file through as he holds it for them. Men will say, simply, "People open doors for other people." Why is it that something so minor can become so symbolic when it happens between a man and a woman?

In the course of interviewing for this book, I asked more than a dozen women how they feel when a man opens a door for them, holds out their chair, rises when they enter a room, walks on the curbside of the sidewalk or other kinds of courtesies boys were trained in from infancy a couple of generations ago.

The fourteen women I asked about this topic range in age from twenty-six to fifty-one. They all said that it was nice when a man did such things, that it made them feel special, cherished or adored, and that they thought more highly of him. However, they almost universally agreed that if the relationship is business, such behavior is insulting. What an interesting dichotomy that is.

Consider, however, what Montagu theorizes in *The Natural Superiority of Women:*

> *Men have brow-beaten women from time immemorial, and one of the subtlest of the ways in which they have done so is through the development of elaborate codes of chivalry and etiquette. The forms of chivalry and etiquette, though they may have been and may continue to be much valued by women, were originally not really intended as friendly acts; they represented the*

behavior of a patronizing superior who, in effect, was saying: "As your superior, I am called upon to give you my support, and make things easier for you. You, as an inferior person, are in all respects less capable than I; and as long as you continue to recognize these facts, and remain submissive and dependent, I will continue to be polite to you." Chivalry was thus a kind of fictitious benevolence, the gloss put by good manners on selfishness, self-conceit, and contempt for the rights of women. Observe how chivalry and the ordinary rules of politeness break down as soon as women begin to compete with men on their own home grounds.

Interestingly, another account of the true origin of chivalric love had nothing at all to do with sex or even the protector-benefactor relationship. It was intended to almost deify the object of one's desire—the woman in most cases—who was generally already married to someone else. The transmutation of love for her into heroic or other deeds, often of service to God (for example, the Crusades of the Middle Ages), was considered a high form of love for another. It is presumed that this was a way of experiencing godly love without the additional mess and fuss of sexual love.

So was the origin of chivalry and gallantry that of a benefactor or a supplicant? Observing historical records indicates it was both. It meant different things to different people, depending on the content of their lives. Have things changed so much?

Are you thoroughly confused now? How do you think guys feel?

When it comes to sex, I think about a comment made by one of my New York friends: "What can a man do for me that I can't do for myself with two C batteries?" So I ask you, do we actually need them, or do we just like them? What is a man's proper place in the world?

In 1792, Mary Wollstonecraft, considered the first of the great feminists, wrote a book called *Vindication of the Rights of Women*. Remember, this was long before we had any rights as a member of the species. In it she says, "Men, in general, seem to employ their reason to justify prejudices, which they have imbibed, they cannot trace how, rather than root them out." Don't we do the same? If we examine it, we do, in certain situations.

Some women delude themselves into believing they cannot buy a house or a nice car, have a baby, or live their lives fully because some man might not like it. They believe the old wives' tale about how nice girls don't make themselves too strong for a man's tastes.

> *You see a lot of smart guys with dumb women, but you hardly ever see a smart woman with a dumb guy.*
>
> ERICA JONG, AUTHOR

We each can point to some late-thirties or early-forties woman who has never married or had children but is very successful in her career. Perhaps we've been among those who tsk-tsk behind her back at "the poor thing" because she can't seem to make a relationship work because she's so "ballsy."

Conversely, we all knew or were "weak" girls like Marie in high school. The tough ones among us, myself included, resented for no apparent reason the clinging vines, the girls whose life goals were to grow up and get married and create a home and family. Perhaps our cynicism and teasing were ill-founded. It was certainly shameful of us, but as I have grown as a woman I have realized that there are truly more people in this world who believe that they are "feminine" only when that femininity is framed by a male. What a price is paid for that belief!

I think of my friend Janine. She has been married to her second husband for twenty-one years. She is a classic clinging vine, and both of her husbands were ready and eager to take the role of protector, provider and ruler of the kingdom. When they first separated, Janine's husband told me, "I have always tried to create a home where she was safe to grow up. She's been immature since I married her." Now she has left the "safety" of her gilded cage to find herself, to "grow up" and become self-actualized. He cannot understand why she is inclined to do it without him. He doesn't see that his response to her neediness is what entrapped her, even though he consciously understands what is happening. She doesn't really understand yet that her sense of neediness is what got her into trouble in the first place. Unless she figures that out, husband number three will be protector and ruler, too.

She keeps saying to him, "I just need to grow and be free." It is not true that she did not have the freedom to break the social stereotype of dependency—we all have that freedom. When she became an adult, she could have chosen to become a woman responsible for herself. Yet she has not been responsible for herself in her lifetime. Like the classic female, she went from daddy to husband one to husband two to being terrified at forty-six to be on her own. It's no wonder men rule us: A substantial portion of our gender believes we are incapable of creating a wholesome, vibrant, successful life on our own. It's no wonder that we create women who sustain the myth of feminine weakness when we consider how many of us assume that neediness and the need to be defended are relationship essentials and that women who do succeed alone are overly masculine and inflexible.

> *I'm not offended by all the dumb blond*
> *jokes because I know I'm not dumb,*
> *and I also know I'm not blond.*
>
> DOLLY PARTON, SINGER

In 1964, Montagu interviewed a young woman who at twenty-five had already been divorced twice. Her entire goal in life was to find someone else to marry and support her. She even told him, "I'm the clinging-vine type." (Surely no modern woman would say that. She would certainly feel guilty if she did.) Montagu sent her to study with a professor he knew and encouraged her to finish college. She became the head of a class of sixty within a short period of time. Did this change her personality? Did she suddenly rejoice in the discovery of her own power? He reports she did not, but that it scared her so badly she remained on the alert for any man but now could not find one.

Brenda, thirty-six and a sales rep, tells me that finding a man is a critical goal in her life. "I really want to get a house. You know, get started living." I ask her why she doesn't get one now, if that's her real goal. "Oh," she explains, "What if it was too far for him to drive from there to his work? Then I'd have to give it up and that'd be hard after putting a lot of time into fixing it up." *She hasn't even met the "right" guy yet!*

Some women start out with the basic presumption that we need men in our lives to feel fulfilled or valuable or whole, that they make us feel like we belong, are worthy, and that only with a man are we really capable of being all we can be. Such women set their lives up consistent with this belief and live their lives gauging their happiness completely on their relationships, or the lack thereof. This toxic basic belief is based on the false assumption that women need men. We can want them, desire them, want to be with them, and recognize the benefits, but we don't *need* them. At the very base of male-female relationships, what do we really need them for physically? The answer is, simply, procreation, and some can contest even that. As a friend of mine says flippantly, "What can a man do for me that I cannot do with a turkey baster and some warm sperm?"

> *Every man I meet wants to protect me from something. I can't figure out what from.*
>
> Mae West, actress, writer

In our society, we have codependent women like Marie, Brenda and Janine, women who float from man to man, waiting to be protected. You know women who are insipid, weak or silly, clinging-vine types, raised or destined to be always protected. Some of them found protectors and lived life in the permanent childlike state, until some inner alarm rang and they realized they had paid for their "safety" with their lives.

At some point, we all stop and wonder, "Hey, is this what I really want?" Maybe that time has come for you now. Neither the extreme of man-hating nor the obsequious behavior related to "need" brings happiness. The real need is to find balance, which comes from the feeling of wholeness as an individual, or as Abraham Maslow says, self-actualization.

If we've been burned, many times we hesitate to get involved with another person in any way other than sexually. We fear losing ourselves in the relationship. Until each of us understands ourselves as truly worthy persons with widely ranging feelings and histories and personality patterns, no man can truly convince us we are worthy of anything. Even nice guys who try to bolster a woman's sagging self-esteem will meet with defeat. Only you can reward yourself with a sense of self-worth. In the absence of that confidence about yourself, you will constantly attract and then rebuff potential partners, and they will never get close enough to see underneath the attractive exterior you create. Underneath all the sweetness or sexiness or whatever you use to hook their interest in the first place, you remain a normal, common, wonderful, terrific, average person, more alike than different from everybody else. When you refuse to allow the growth of intimacy—knowing who the other person is and exposing yourself—the result is always loneliness, even in a relationship. (This is why we must learn to be impeccable in our speech. It is the first platform of intimacy!)

While it is true that we cannot force one another into the same mold—indeed, that would be boring—it is certainly true that our culture, our media and our generational memories still encourage us to perceive ourselves as less than equal, as needing or requiring a man to be complete. As Tessa Warschaw says, some of us still believe a single woman is as useless as a matchless sock.

These stories illuminate the old adage "It's more important to *be* the right person than to *find* the right person." Still we scurry from man to man, confident only that eventually we'll find the right one. We make decisions to settle down when we get tired of scurrying. We give up on the search, never realizing it is an inner search, never realizing the truth in the statement "We attract what we are, not what we want." First, we must invest our energy in personal growth. Only then can we look for a mate, when we have developed sufficient self-confidence and clarity about who we are.

Once we have taken a time-out from frenetic sexual activity and have developed our own self-worth, we have a much better chance of finding, attracting and maintaining a healthy relationship with a suitable partner. We have a much better chance of deciding if we even *want* a man. Don't you agree with this logical statement? While we know we will never meet our ideal of personal perfection, at the same time, constantly getting bad results in relationships might be an indicator that we need to work on internal matters to attract better circumstances externally. It takes time to get to know ourselves and time to get to know the men we date. Can we afford that time? Yes, indeed we can, because we cannot afford to continue living our lives without investing that time.

So what good conclusion can we draw from the fact that we do not specifically need men, or that we can choose not to need them, or that we can choose to want them, or not want them— as we see fit? Although there are stereotypical norms, although there is social pressure, there is no reason to settle for anything less than what you want from yourself, your life or men. By the power of your own mind, you have the power to create precisely what you want in your outer world. That may include an ideal relationship, and for most readers, it probably will. It also might include some time in the company of born-again virgins.

What else can we deduce from the realization that we don't need men? For one, they don't need us either. They can come into their own and live full lives without us. (Albeit we think they are less likely to do so without a woman's prodding.)

While I was writing this chapter, a male friend called and joked, "If all the women died tomorrow, within six months every man would be unshaven, have long unkempt hair and a pot belly, and drink a lot more beer. However, if all the men died tomorrow, six months later the whole place would look great, there'd be more flowers, better day-care centers, it'd be more peaceful, and the women would still get dressed up and shave their legs." Nonetheless, the basic human needs of food, clothing and shelter can be fulfilled by either sex with or without the presence of the opposite sex. Now that we all know that, can we be confident in our equality? If we are confident, we can choose to want to be with men from a position of strength instead of weakness. We can decide not to sell out, give up or, worst of all, settle. Remember this important tip: You *always* get what you settle for.

It seems that we have evolved consciously far faster than our bodies have evolved since we still have specialized male or female parts. Until and unless our bodies catch up with our minds, we cannot begin to wholly lay aside the physical boundary of gender and become completely self-sufficient on our own, and in any case, that may not be a desirable state. Until the time those differences are nil, however, "we" are forced to get along with "them," and in doing so we must use all the capabilities of our incredibly advanced minds and proceed in this dangerous area with the greatest amount of discernment and reverence for ourselves and the men with whom we interact.

As Rodney King said during a statement after the L.A. riots, "Why can't we all just get along?" I observe that the key to our social development is to enter consciously into like-minded relationships with self-actualizing men and women. I believe we are again redefining what sort of general interaction we want with the other half of the species. I believe the women who choose to become born-again virgins show the foresight to begin walking in the right direction and that in their wake will come greater positive social changes than we have seen in generations.

FIVE

A How-Not-To Crash Course on Love

I think, therefore I'm single.

LIZZ WINSTEAD, COMEDIENNE

Investing in yourself as a person requires courage to face where you are and where you are going. It's living with just yourself in the quiet times between relationships that scares many people. Becoming a BAV can give you space to teach yourself how to love yourself more, to find out who you really are, to find out how to cherish yourself so you can either live happily singly or in a couple relationship. It means getting healthy. It means pulling out the weeds to make room for the flowers in your heart.

Instantly weeding out inappropriate people is not easy, but for the sake of your future, your children if you have or will have them, and your mental and physical well-being, it's critical that you learn how to screen out the losers before you get hurt. Beginning with your external world, you can make changes internally. Growth can start outside or inside.

Chances are you've been hurt. Chances are you've hit bottom in your dating life. Chances are you've cried a few tears over your own loneliness, inability to connect with the right person, regret over past mistakes or health problems from past mistakes. The good news is, as psychiatrists say, "When it hurts enough, you'll change."

If you believe that you would be a more complete person, moving closer to your goals, happier, healthier and attaining whatever else you seek in your life, isn't it logical to conclude that that is true only if you find and maintain the ideal relationship with yourself first? You can't do that when you're looking to some albatross hanging around your neck to help you. Doesn't it also follow that you could have avoided the bozos you've dated if from day one you'd listened to your instincts and not your hormones? You can learn to listen to those instincts from the peaceful inner sanctum of the born-again virgin.

She's a Modern Woman

Kersten is a modern woman. She's a professional schoolteacher and a never-married single mother of a thirteen-year-old son. When she conceived him during her junior year at college, she was "just sort of dating" his father. At that moment, she was surprised but confident in herself. She made the decision to leave the country she was in and raise the child alone. Here's her story:

"When I was in my twenties, I would get involved on the first date. Everybody did then. Then I read a book about games to play to get a husband, sort of like *The Rules* now. I've never been able to do that, though. I like someone or I don't. I don't play games."

Kersten paused for a few moments. It was taking a lot of courage to verbalize beliefs she holds about herself. "I feel men like the game of anticipation. When you don't give them [the game], they never get excited. They seem to get bored faster. I think if I'd followed [this game], I would have gotten a man. *I might not be happy, but at least I'd have someone.*"

I think about her words as she speaks them. "Games." "Rules." It's like we need to trick them into wanting us when they already do naturally. It's giving up our true power. It's like there is a big competition going on and we're all competing for the same prize. Look around. How many of your girlfriends' husbands or boyfriends are you *really* jealous of? Are they men you'd sincerely like to be with, or would you be unhappy, as perhaps your friends are, but "at least you'd have someone." Are the men you know the prize you seek?

Kersten is remarkably self-aware. She tells me, "I'm still not playing games and I'm still getting the same results. I think a marriage started with games creates a marriage of games. I'd rather be lonely than unhappy. I told my ex-fiancé that, because he said I'd be lonely when I left him."

Kersten doesn't hear the discrepancies in her thinking while she's speaking to me, but her current lifestyle supports *"I'd rather be lonely than unhappy."* I venture she could be happy single or married. She's moving in that direction. She tells me how the last man she dated never tried to change who she is, just let her be and appreciated her as she is right now. "I am a person who tries to fit the mold. He never tried to change me. It proves men are capable of that."

Kersten is experimenting with her life choices. She's considering her true values as she examines them in her own heart and head, instead of in a relationship—good or bad. As she grows into more delight and joy in who she is and how she's managed her life so far, she will probably come to see herself as attractive, desirable and, by all means, self-confident. This factor in itself will attract men to her.

Kersten has made a life for herself and her child. She has a successful career, enough food to eat, a good relationship with her child, friends. She's living proof that we can do it alone, like so many modern women are doing. She might not sound ecstatic about her choices, but they are hers alone and she can make new ones at any time.

Take my friend Susan. She's had a long-distance romance with a guy in Kentucky for about two years. He flies out to her home in Colorado once a month or so. Suddenly, he got offered a transfer to Denver—two hours from her house. Here's a man she has been faithful to for two years, a man she calls her boyfriend to all males wondering if she—a vivacious, attractive, bright woman—is available. You'd think she would be ecstatic he's moving. Her reaction shocked me. "I'm not sure I like him enough to see him more often," she said. After two years, what a waste of energy! She could have decided long ago she didn't really want to be in a relationship with him at this time in her life or ever again and acted on it. She could have dated him nonexclusively or preferably not at all and spent her time investigating where the right person for her is. She could have invested that energy in her ten-year-old son or in learning karate or pinochle or tap dancing, or improving her life, personality or health. Susan's hit bottom.

Instead, she did what so many of us do when we feel guilty and scared but want to end the relationship anyway. In the name of "making it easier on the other person," she became, as Susan calls her behavior toward this poor guy, "the bitch from hell." We make ourselves so undesirable, so mean-spirited, so rude, that eventually the guy just has to abandon us. I suspect most of us have done that at least once or twice. At least that way we avoided telling him, "Look, I know I've been sleeping with you, but in reality, you aren't right for me, so please get lost." We also get to assume the guy feels happier because he's the one breaking up instead of us. (P.S.: Men don't seem to think like we do about this subject.)

Love's a disease, but curable.
Did you ever look through a microscope
at a drop of pond water? You see plenty of
love there. All the amoebae getting married.
I presume they think it very exciting
and important. We don't.

DAME ROSE MACAULAY, ENGLISH NOVELIST

What are you really giving up when you hit bottom and stay there in your relationships? The answer is your life, one wasted moment at a time. Time is each person's primary nonrenewable resource and, therefore, most precious. I don't know about you, but before I became a BAV, my life went something like this:

Spend time in a bad relationship.

Worry for a while how to get out of it.

Get out of it and spend time feeling either sorry for myself or guilty for the guy I thought I hurt.

Start looking around for a new relationship. (Read: time usually wasted.)

Repeat cycle.

Each one of these phases cost me precious time, as well as energy and focus on other things. Many of the women I spoke to while preparing this book admit they spend a lot of time on relationships: beginning them, living them, ending and finding new ones. The cycle is incredibly costly in terms of human energy. I know I was crashing through my life, looking for love. Have you done that, too?

Think for a moment about how precious your time is. If you work for someone else, forty hours or more each week of your life are dedicated to his or her needs, at least in theory. If you are a mom, you're on full-time duty except two weekends a month when your ex has the kids. If you make a commitment to keep in shape, you have to spend time exercising. You want to take a painting class, read that new book you bought or organize your Tupperware collection—but there's never enough time.

Further, every day you're alive is not only the first day of the rest of your life, it is also one day closer to your last. (Okay, so that's morbid, but isn't it true?) Given that these things are true and that no matter how much more life you want you cannot buy, beg, borrow or steal a minute more, then time is your most precious commodity.

I've been on so many blind dates, I should get a free dog.

WENDY LIEBMAN, COMEDIENNE

If time is all you really have to spend, then doesn't it follow that deciding how you spend that time is the most critical decision you can make on a, well, on a minute-by-minute basis? The things you do today, the people you spend time with, the activities you participate in determine not only the quality of your life today but also determine, in most cases, the quality of your life in the future, too. Aren't you worthy of using your time in the best possible way? Of course you are.

If you are a persistently grumpy, irritable, stressed-out mom because you don't have enough time, there's a good chance you are creating problems for yourself that will manifest when your kids become teenagers or leave home early to get away from you. On the brighter side, if you decide to spend your time taking a night class, you could conceivably change careers and create an amazing economic future for yourself in a profession you love. My friend Mark Victor Hansen tells of a woman who came up to him after a seminar and said she couldn't go back to college because it would take five years and she'd be forty-two when she got out. Mark asked her how old she'd be in five years if she didn't go back to college. If you spend your time dating or, worse, sleeping next to guys with whom you have no future because they don't treat you right, you create lowered self-esteem for yourself and a sense of unhappiness that will make it harder to get into a good relationship in the future, to create the whole life you want, whatever that is. It will drain you, tiny bit by tiny bit.

Your time is all you have. You are ultimately in charge of how you use it. The people and activities that demand your time demand it because you allow the demand. Crashing through relationships or wasting time in wrong ones is sucking your life away. Stop! Stop right now!

Planting Hope

In spring, I get passionate about seeds—almost any kind of seeds: vegetable, flower, even tree seeds, especially the seeds of trees that could never possibly grow in my climate, it seems, and I spend a few weekends turning over my garden, planning where to plant and then planting these seeds. When the seedlings poke through the soil, the work begins and the fun for me ends. I know it will cost me about four times as much per tomato to harvest those I've planted as to buy the organic ones at the store. I know that I dislike trying to fit in time for watering and weeding. Most of all, I hate the bugs a garden attracts. But every springtime, I happily invest the time to plant the seeds. I choose to plant them and commit to nurturing them to mature plants, even though I don't like all the parts of the process. As I write this mid-March, a light rain is falling on row upon row of germinating seeds in my too large garden. I recognize that I chose to invest this time. I also recognize that four months from now, I will be complaining about the amount of work it takes to have a garden. Still, each spring the choice is mine, isn't it? I know full well the outcome. I know which parts I like and which ones I don't. After all, it's my time, and it's my life. I recognize that my conscious conclusion is "Even though I dislike parts of this, the compromise is worth it."

My garden is like some women's attitudes toward men. They like the early part, when everyone is on their best behavior and things are all full of promise—like my seeds before they become a chore—but when it comes to the constant maintenance, nurturing, caring for, tending and protecting from weeds, the garden loses its luster a bit—or the man does. Then it's time to focus on finding another man, then another, always hoping for the elusive one who stays perennially full of promise and hope. There is no such garden and there is no such life, yet we often continue to plant our seeds in the wrong soil, or we garden when we should be doing something more in alignment with our true goals.

The Bible has a parable called "The Sower" that also provides a useful metaphor for this behavior: A farmer was planting seeds. Some fell on the road and the birds ate them. Some fell on the rocks, where the soil was shallow, and they sprouted quickly but also died quickly because they had no depth into which to sink their roots. Some fell into the thistles and were choked out by thorns. Some fell on good soil and produced an excellent harvest. In other words, the farmer was 25 percent effective. I think this story should be called "The Parable of the Foolish Farmer" (although some scholars believe the story is about how people receive religion), but it applies to the women who are haphazard about the men with whom they get involved.

What's interesting about this parable for me is how it seems to apply to relationships. Some relationships never take root and no one knows why. The "birds" of life swoop down and eat up a little spark here or the guy over there moves away right after he asks for your phone number. Then there are the relationships that don't have much depth, like crushes—the wow! parts of romance and attraction. They're those that sprout and die fast. There are also those relationships that never really work out because they're ignored for other priorities, such as work, perhaps kids, and other responsibilities. Such relationships get choked out by life, and many marriages end this way, having taken root but not making it out of the thorns. Finally, 25 percent of the seeds you've sown produce what you really want. The soil is great, the seeds are healthy, and they land in the right place—if you're lucky.

Sleeping around, or sleeping with someone you really don't know well enough, is also kind of like those seeds. At best, you have a 25-percent chance of payoff. Why doesn't the farmer in the story, or you in your life, take the time to dig a furrow and plant the seed where it will have optimum opportunity for growth? The answer, probably, is that it requires time. It's easier to just toss the seeds up in the air and see where they land and what happens. However, a logical, careful farmer would select the optimum soil, plant the highest quality seed, put the germinating seed in the best location and make sure the soil stayed moist. In relationships, we sometimes choose poorly or try to grow the entirely wrong seeds, and the soil, which is our hearts, isn't ready to grow anything yet because we haven't healed.

Half the divorced women reading this book probably floated down the aisle without a reservation in their heads for anything other than the honeymoon suite. Regardless, we're older, smarter and wiser now. We're mature women, competent, able to take care of ourselves. The women's revolution, the feminist movement, has given us power and freedom and all the attendant responsibilities. We owe it to ourselves, our daughters and our sisters to make sure we're planting our seeds in the best possible soil.

Thankfully, the feminist revolution has had a wonderful effect on women's rights. For the first time in history, women in the United States simultaneously have the ability, the access to education, and the drive to create economic independence for themselves. The remains of the generational stigma of needing a man are fading. The concept of relationship choice is taking precedence. Choice implies that the chooser is aware of what she wants and makes choices based on criteria she has established for herself, much as she picks out a good tomato at the grocery store: Is this a store that stocks good produce? Have I gotten good tomatoes here in the past? Are tomatoes in season? Is the color right? Are these tomatoes plump enough? Red enough? Do I want hydroponic or hothouse tomatoes? Are they bruised, grayish or mealy? Do they look fresh and alive or dull and dying?

Sowing the Seeds of Time

We would never sit at home waiting for the ideal tomato to come to us. How preposterous it is that we do our shopping without selection criteria for something so much more important.

I suspect many divorced women now wonder what they were thinking when they married. It takes time to get to know a person. A generation ago, the advice was to date through at least all four seasons of the year before making a choice about marrying.

This provided time to see potential mates in different situations, to compare them to your ideal, and to consider how they meshed with your own sense of self and your personal values and interests. The Chinese oracle, the I Ching, has taught people for thousands of years to recognize there are seasons in nature and in ourselves and to work with them, not against.

The reality of the new millennium is that more and more women *and* men are wearying of the relentless pressure to be sexual early—before they even know the person with whom they are getting naked. Meaningful sex can only come "in due season."

It appears that as much as we protest, and as much as we are told casual sex is possible, frankly it isn't. If you've noticed this, you are not alone. Think about the last few relationships you've been in that didn't work out. At the end, did you think "If I had known then what I know now, I would never have begun anything with him"? Guess what? Becoming a born-again virgin can guarantee (or your money back) that you will never have to experience that thought again.

With men, moving too quickly into sex blurs your ability to evaluate your selection before you buy. As every woman knows, once most couples start having sex, they automatically have it every time they are together, which really cuts down on conversation. They stop finding out how they can grow as friends and stop taking as much time to focus on their individual growth. They find out less about what the other person thinks and more about how they perform as a lover. It's fun in the moment, but marriages based purely on hormones are in for some tough times ahead. As Lisa said, "You know if someone has a birthmark on their butt before you know if they have a kind and open heart."

Obviously, we want to be sexually compatible with someone we choose as a life partner or with whom we create a long-term dating relationship. However, all too often we become lovers with someone we aren't even sure we really like as a person, or the veneer we project in the early days of courtship wears off, and we find we kissed the prince and he became a toad. For a variety of reasons we end up sleeping in the wrong bed and waking up next to a stranger. Then to get out of the relationship we're in we have to expend time and energy that otherwise could have been used to find and develop ourselves and also a relationship with Mr. Right.

> *His mother should have thrown him away and kept the stork.*
>
> MAE WEST, ACTRESS, WRITER

Another important point is that when we rush into a relationship, we are consigned to live in fear of getting hurt. Martha, a BAV and a banker, said she waited almost six months before she became sexual with her current boyfriend, with whom she's now been exclusive for two years. She had known him for about seven years before they became sexually active. "I think when you rush into it, you risk getting disappointed," Martha explained. "Because for a woman, you believe you're giving part of yourself when you have sex."

Martha believes that women today find themselves giving away more and getting less. She said women have sex with a man and then think, "I gave you part of myself. Now what are you going to give me?" These expectations support every reason to wait. Regarding even her current relationship, Martha says, "I don't want to get my hopes up." Martha is a woman who knows what she's in this for—and that very fact means she's self-actualizing.

The way to reduce your chances of crashing in love is to enter into sexuality slowly. Take your time. Get to know him first. Be honest with him and yourself.

The Tale of the Celibate Lesbian Nun

In biblical times,
a man could have as many
wives as he could afford.
Just like today.

ABIGAIL VAN BUREN, COLUMNIST

She said, "I'm a celibate lesbian nun!" When I laughed and asked her what that meant, she said, "It's like this: I'm a lesbian because I don't want to have sex with any men. I'm celibate because I truly don't want to have sex with any women. And I'm a nun because I need a good reason for it all!"

This book gives women "a good reason for it all"—without joining a convent. Bad reasons, good reasons, other people's reasons and your own reasons for becoming a BAV are available, if you want them. What might stopping the sex game mean to you? This book gives you a chance to pause and consider if celibacy might be right for you—for a week, a month, a year or a lifetime.

Previous chapters have presented the facts surrounding taking time to think through your life and your relationships, your choices and the results of those choices. You've read about changing the way you behave and the way you think about yourself and your sexuality. What else can you gain from making the choice to become a BAV?

One of the most amazing things about consciously controlling your sexuality is gaining the power to focus. Think about a time you really, really wanted something. Didn't you focus most of your energy on that goal until it was reached? Whether you wanted to finish school, learn to drive a car, prepare for a test or do something as simple as shopping, you had to devote mental resources to it—you had to direct your energy toward that goal. If it was accomplished, you had to focus on it until completion.

The bigger the goal, the more energy it requires. It takes a lot of focus to decide in high school you will become a doctor and then to follow through. It takes far less focus and commitment to remember to buy milk and a loaf of bread on your way home. Still, for every goal to be attained, you must apply conscious effort for some period of time, however brief.

Remember the list in chapter 1, the list of benefits other women have achieved by becoming conscious and connected to their sexuality again? Go back and take a look at the things you marked down. Remind yourself what made you keep reading this book in the first place. This is where you start to apply all you've learned in the preceding chapters to your daily life. This chapter is about how that all works.

For example, a major goal of mine was obtaining the first house I bought four years after my divorce—the one I live in now. My daughter and I were living in a too-small apartment, and I knew I needed space of my own. I spent a year looking at houses, reading real estate magazines and for-sale ads and signs, exploring neighborhoods, and searching for the right house. I finally found a great place in an ideal neighborhood. I made an offer. The seller refused it. I was upset, but I countered. I couldn't understand why things weren't going my way. I was quite close to the seller's dollar figure, but he did not let me buy it, despite my three counteroffers. It made no sense. It turned out later that that house needed extreme structural repairs. If I had ended up with that one, we would have been miserable.

A few months later, when it worked out that I got twice the house on two lots with a great view for about the same price, I felt like my focus and ability to not give up in discouragement had really paid off. I love my home! Ironically, that first house is literally right next door, a frequent reminder of what a close call that was. The guy who did buy it is quite handy and happy as can be.

I focused on what I wanted, I was as prepared as I thought I could be, I did my homework, I knew what I could afford and I had my down payment ready. When the seller turned me down, it surprised and hurt me, but through the 20/20 of hindsight, I can see that it all worked out for the best. To use the seed analogy again, I worked out the ideal conditions by focusing on my desired result.

I'm telling you this story for several reasons: First, you are preparing yourself for the next stage of your life, whatever that may be, by becoming a BAV. Good for you! It's similar to the homework I did on real estate. Second, you are taking time now to think about whether or not you want a relationship and, if you do, what that would look like for you. I wrote my goals down for the house: It had to have a fireplace, a nice yard, a guesthouse and room for an office, among other things. This was important because it helped me weed out inappropriate houses before I wasted time looking at, say, mobile homes or condos. It works that way with men, too. If you screen them at once against what you want, you won't waste any time. Third, even though I was as ready financially, emotionally and mentally as I could be to buy the first house, the seller had to be ready to sell it. He wasn't, and there was nothing I could do about that, short of meeting his unreasonable demands. So, although I was hurt, I walked away from the deal. You can figure out the parallel to relationships all by yourself, I'm sure.

In the end, I got the right house by consistently focusing on my goal. I didn't give up when I failed once. I didn't generalize that all houses are crummy and all sellers idiots. I took stock and went back into the ring—and I won.

The power of focus is the fuel that gets each of us our goals when we apply it. If I had been distracted in my search for a house by thinking "Oh, maybe I should settle for a condo or a mobile home," I could have ended up with something I really didn't want. (Not that there is anything intrinsically wrong with either of those housing options.) This works the same way in relationships, jobs, health, weight—everything. You get exactly what you focus on, whether that is lack or abundance. You also get exactly what you settle for. Remember the meditation I offered you? In it, you start with gratitude, which encourages your mind to enjoy the abundance you already experience! It helps you *focus* on abundance and what's positive.

In the movie *Elizabeth,* Elizabeth I of England is burned in love, and she learns the hard way not to trust romantic allegiances. Her kingdom is falling apart, she is being pressured to marry on every front, and in due course she decides to refrain from involvement with men and become a virgin. While the true story of Elizabeth I is somewhat different from that portrayed in the movie (apparently she really did remain a virgin from birth), the historical reality of her life is the same as the fictionalization: She chose to refrain from marriage and sexual intercourse in order to more clearly focus her energy and power on ruling her country.

Elizabeth I chose not to settle down with the King of Spain, the Duke of France, or other world leaders and apparently chose celibacy as her lifestyle. Her true intention seems clear to those who observe her through the window of history: She made a conscious decision to focus on the things most important to her. She often voiced her belief that marriage would be superfluous for her. The historical record (not the movie) quotes her as having said, "I would rather be a beggar and single than a queen and married. . . . I should call the wedding ring the yoke ring."

Elizabeth I believed marriage's restrictions and its bounds were best disowned for the sake of ruling the country. Was she right? Did she make the right choice for herself—this queen of the born-again virgins? During her reign, England became a vast trading empire, a formidable world power, and one of the wealthiest countries in the world with one of the highest standards of living. She is attributed with inducting England's

"Golden Age." She used her "free time" to create a vast empire. Could this have been a direct result of Elizabeth's decision to hone her focus?

Very few of us have the choice to build our country into a world power. Very few of us experience the convenience of having legions of servants cater to our whims if we choose to marry or remarry. Still, how many of us stop to consider the options we do or might have while single or married? How many of us stop to think about the fact that responsibilities and sacrifices inherent in a relationship can make achieving all of our goals more difficult? Conversely, are there goals that we each could reach more easily if we were in the right relationship? How do we each figure out what's right for us right now?

> *It is sad that my emotional dependence on the man I love should have killed so much of my energy and ability; there was certainly once a great deal of energy in me.*
>
> SONYA TOLSTOY, WIFE OF LEO TOLSTOY

Is a relationship really something you want right now? Society pressures us to say "Yes!" but if you're the one sabotaging your relationships, it could be it's because you don't really want to be in one. (Of course, you could be sabotaging from fear, too. Only you truly know about that.)

Let's pretend you don't really want a relationship for a moment, for now or forever. What else might you want?

The top position in your company

To own your own company

To be a millionaire before you enter your next decade of living

To buy/pay off your home

To raise a child in the freedom that can exist without a partner

To cure cancer or leukemia or AIDS

To follow Jane Goodall's trail to help gorillas

To spend a year in the Peace Corps

To become a lesbian

To invent something

To write a book

To change careers

There are six billion things you can do with your life. Many you can do if you're in the right relationship, but guess what? You're not. And you're alive anyway. So you may as well apply yourself to creating the life you want right now, and if you get a relationship you want to keep, terrific. If you don't, at least you'll love your life.

It's okay not to want to be with someone right now. It's okay to want to be with someone. It's okay to want to be with some-one special later—like after your kids leave home or you finish your degree. It's your life. It's going fast. Get it while you can.

Let's try a short goal-setting exercise. Find yourself a quiet place and take a piece of paper and a pen. With minimal intro-spection, write down your first answers to the following ques-tions. You can go back and twiddle with what you write down later. Right now, get down your first answers. You may have twenty immediate responses and a hundred more tomorrow when you've thought about it more, or you may have just one big response. Whatever comes up for you is just fine.

> Question One: What would you do with your life if someone gave you $5 million today?
>
> Question Two: You've just talked to your doctor. You have six months to live. How will you spend the end of your time?
>
> Question Three: You're turning eighty years old and friends and family are hosting a "This Is Your Life" party for you. What do they list among your many accomplishments?
>
> Question Four: What would you do if you knew absolutely that you could not fail?

These questions will get you started thinking about what your real goals are. You may surprise yourself with your answers. If you come back to this in six months and do it again, you may find your goals are the same and stronger, or completely different, or you may experience the delight of realizing you have taken steps that have brought you closer to the goals you wrote today. You go, girl!

The Queen of De-Nile

We find another wonderful example of focus in the ancient story of Cleopatra. In *The Warrior Queens: The Legends and the Lives of the Women Who Have Led Their Nations in War*, that excellent British historian Antonia Fraser reports, "The picture we do have is of a Cleopatra who was not only strong-minded but ambitious enough to have her own conception of empire. . . . A close inspection of Cleopatra's career reveals far more concentration on power politics and far less self-indulgent dalliance than wishful popular imagination cares to admit. Whether beautiful or not (she has a heavy if sultry look to the modern eye) Cleopatra certainly understood how to make the best use of her fascinating femininity."

My own favorite historical woman, Mary, Queen of Scots, is often touted as an ingenue haplessly tripping from one romantic and political mishap to another. Yet a truer understanding than can be gleaned from current romantic writing shows a woman who was consistently true to the values she held. Were she merely the silly girl she is frequently portrayed as, surely her powerful and wily cousin, Elizabeth I, would have had no interest in contending with the political dilemma of severing Mary's "foolish" head. From my own extensive studies of Mary, I conclude that she judged incorrectly but nonetheless applied all her skills toward ruling her empire in alignment with her religious beliefs while trying desperately to combine it with romantic satisfaction. She was self-actualizing based on her own goals.

These women all achieved their greatness by focusing on their goals. Sometimes, when we look at the great women of history, we see that many who have become powerful in their own right rarely have a man behind them. I saw a bumper sticker the other day that said, "Behind every successful woman is . . . herself." Is there a truer statement? Perhaps only this one: "Behind almost every woman you ever heard of stands a man who let her down."

So we've got brains, drive, guts and sexual energy coming out our ears—and other orifices. It hasn't always been like this, you know. In 1912, Lady Alice Hillingdon voiced a fairly typical viewpoint on women's sexuality. She wrote to a friend, "I am happy now that Charles calls on my bedchamber less frequently than of old. As it is I now endure but two calls a week and when I hear his steps outside my door, I lie down on my bed, close my eyes, open my legs and think of England."

Victorian England, responding culturally perhaps to the Puritan viewpoint that preceded it, denounced sex as carnal and evil and simply wanted to deny it existed or ever happened. Sex with your spouse was seen then as bestial. Egregious numbers of abortions and whorehouses abounded in Victorian London as witness to the reality of this "nonexistent" sexual urge. Men were not supposed to impose sexual feelings on their wives. Ladies simply didn't want sex. Enter Freud, who finally stated that extreme sexual repression was unhealthy.

Millions of ladylike women lived and died without orgasms, without finding pleasure in the sexual act. Thankfully, this out-rage was overcorrected in the 1960s and 1970s through the work of American feminists such as Gloria Steinem and Betty Friedan. Hurrah for them! They showed us that we are every bit as sexual—perhaps more—than men. Thank you, ladies! We've had fun. We had permission at last to go out and wrap ourselves around any penis we wanted. In fact, we were odd if we didn't. Women had finally broken through the Victorian prudery Lady Alice Hillingdon and her set lived through. Now we have come as far as men, who have apparently never doubted the intensity of their sexual nature. Now it's time we proceed.

As we take it a step further and consider the fact that we now know we have this potent sexual power, let's use our superior intellect to harness it to create equality, to create a matriarchal society, to end hunger, to end war, to divert some of the money spent on arms toward healing disease, to gain peace and to make sure that the homeless, the sick, the insane and the little children of the world have a safe place to sleep tonight. Let's use it to fund the projects that are dearest to women's hearts. Let's use our sexual power, not suppress it, not overwhelm ourselves with the gluttony of it. Let's harness it. Let's go places! What social and personal changes could we create?

> *When women are depressed,*
> *they eat or go shopping. Men invade*
> *another country.*
>
> ELAYNE BOOSLER, COMEDIENNE

Women: The Gentler Gender?

In *The Warrior Queens,* Antonia Fraser also raises the point that women may or may not be inclined toward a more pacifistic world. On page 7 she points out, "Part of . . . [the] fear or admiration [paid to women who start or rule wars] is undoubtedly due to the fact that woman as a whole has been seen as a pacifying influence throughout history, this pacifying role being perceived as hers by nature and hers in duty. The whole question of whether women actually *are* more pacific by nature is not the subject of the present book. . . . Some feminist writers have recently strongly promulgated the notion that a matriarchal society would or did lack the aggression that does and did characterize a patriarchal one. (Evidently nonpacific types such as Mrs. Gandhi, Mrs. Meir and Mrs. Thatcher count as honorary men for the purposes of this argument because they have adopted masculine views in order to succeed in the patriarchal world.)" Fraser also quotes Lynne Segal, author of *Is the Future Female?* as saying, "I accept that women are gentler at the moment," but "if they had the same amount of power as men, they wouldn't be more virtuous."

Fraser and Segal bring up an interesting point. They wonder what would happen if women had the same power as men, if we would use it in the same way they have for violence and victory. The question boils down to what we would do individually and collectively with power once we had it.

The social evolution toward celibacy and abstinence is happening all around us, and through our feminine power, we are already subjugating what has proven to be an oppressive patriarchy. By insisting on our standards instead of allowing men to set the standard, we create the opportunity not only for harmony between the sexes but also, if we collectively choose it, for the opportunity to oppress men.

I believe the answer to the question of what we will choose remains individual. There are women who will perceive the message in this book as one of man-hating ball-busting. There are others who will find it a sweet tome on revering our bodies. In reality, it is both and neither. This is a walk in the garden: You don't have to like every flower, bee and thorn you find there, but the very experience of becoming aware of the variety will lead you into a place of greater knowledge and, with it, greater choice, because knowledge is power after all.

Celibacy and sex are two sides of the same whole. Each is made valuable only by choice. If you cannot choose to be freely celibate, it follows that you do not have any choice about your sexuality. Each act of sex, whether partaken of or refrained from, must be done with choice.

Elizabeth I, Cleopatra, Catherine the Great of Russia and many other powerful females, had a true lust for power. I can only assume that the lust for power included a lust for sex, as it does in many men and women who seek and attain great power. The men of history have traditionally been blamed less than women for their sexual roving, including Elizabeth I's own father (Henry VIII) and Thomas Jefferson and others all the way to Bill Clinton, all men of great power as well as great sexual energy. The two traits seem to go hand in hand. The conclusion must be that they chose to subjugate some of that power for political power. You can use that same power to create whatever it is you want in your life. You can use that same sexual power to meet your goals.

Napoleon Hill wrote a famous book called *Think and Grow Rich.* I am privileged to own a 1947 edition published by the Ralston Society in Cleveland. (I hear the Ralstons left publishing and went on to make marvelous dog food!) Hill's benefactor, Andrew Carnegie, assigned him the task of interviewing the most influential men of his time. (Influential women weren't taken into account at the time.) Among many other traits for success, Hill found that intense sexual power or prowess is a hallmark of successful men—not because they use it but because they control it and direct its energy to their own purposes. A whole section of the book is dedicated to the concept of *sexual transmutation,* by which Hill implies that sexual drive—the more intense the better—can be mastered by will for the sake of success, power or fame. I paraphrase: "Sex desire is the most powerful of human desires. . . . When harnessed, and redirected along other lines, this motivating force maintains all of its attributes of keenness of imagination, courage [will power, persistence and creative ability] which may be used as powerful creative forces in literature, art, or in any other profession or calling, including, of course, the accumulation of riches."

"The transmutation [transferring, changing] of sex energy calls for an exercise of will power, to be sure, but the reward is worth the effort. . . . The desire cannot and should not be submerged or eliminated. But it should be given an outlet through forms of expression which enrich the body, mind, and spirit of [wo]man[kind]. . . . A river may be dammed, and its water controlled, but eventually it will force an outlet. The same is true for the emotion of sex. . . . Fortunate indeed is the person who has discovered how to give sex emotion an outlet through some form of creative effort, for [s]he has, by that discovery, lifted [herself] to the status of a genius."

Okay, okay, sign me up! I want to be a genius: a happy, attractive, wealthy, balanced genius with lots of friends and a good life. So how do we do it—or in this case, not do it? If I am convinced that becoming a born-again virgin is right for me, how do I live it? What benefits can I hope to achieve from my decision, beyond the hope that I will attract a better relationship?

Victoria St. George, forty-five, a professional writer and a BAV since her relationship ended four years ago, said, "Not being in a relationship has made me more aware of sexual energy in others. I quickly see 'couple energy' and I see people with 'on the lookout' energy, and I see how people sublimate those energies. I think everyone needs to express it. I do it by dancing and by really focusing myself on [my professional life]." Victoria added, "You can be tied into knots by your sexual energy or you can use it in any other way."

As a highly creative person, Victoria found she can turn it into creative energy to enhance the production of the many books she works on in a year (some of which have been bestsellers). Great writers, painters and other creatives throughout history have claimed that diverting their sexual energy into their creative projects has given them an edge. Many basketball, baseball and other pro athletes will not have sex before the game to "save strength" for the game.

How do we transmute sexual energy into a better life? In order to learn to use sexual energy for other purposes, we must first understand what it is and how we generate it.

Our brain is our largest sex organ and also the nuclear reactor that generates pure sexual energy. The "chemistry" we feel when we see someone attractive happens in our brain first (even if the chemicals move much lower in a split second).

This chemistry or "energy of sexual attraction" is empirical in nature. That is, the way it enters us is through one of the five senses or as the thought memory of a previous sensory experience.

The act of recognizing this instant is the first step in harnessing it for your purposes. When the sexual energy becomes conscious, it can be consciously stored and/or focused on your goal.

This is done by mentally replacing the sexual thought with the thought of your goal, something like "Hmmm. He has a nice butt! <beat> I can't wait to make the Million Dollar Roundtable at work!"

If this seems silly to you, it's because you haven't tried it. The strongest positive emotions we encounter are pleasurable: sex, affection, love, happiness, etc. Attaching these strong positive emotions to a future event compels you toward it as fast as you can go. Your brain is driven by pain and pleasure. Attach enough of one or the other to your own actions and thoughts, and you will compel yourself in the direction you want to go.

The shorter the time between the sexual thought and the conscious goal thought, the stronger the association. It's like housebreaking a puppy. If you find the dog poop or chewed-up shoe three hours later, good luck trying to get the dog to associate your displeasure with its behavior. If you catch the dog in the act and immediately link displeasure to its actions, the training process will be short. This is because the dog pretty much lives for your pleasure—a scratch behind the ears, a compliment and so on.

Your brain works at a much more sophisticated level, of course, but the time between the action and the result determines the efficacy of the results of your diverting and harnessing your powerful sexual energy.

Some people fritter away all their sexual power with physical diversions. If the focus of these activities is denial, as in "I'm jogging like a maniac so I'll stop wanting sex!" you're missing the serene benefit of being a BAV. You don't need sex to survive, although you may want it, but want is generated in the brain. Physical action to suppress this desire will backfire and intensify it, because it directs the brain to pay attention to what's missing. When the brain perceives lack, it scrambles to supply it. If you attach energy to a conscious thought, you actually propel yourself to find a way to achieve that thought.

You can store the physical energy expended during the sex act to increase athletic performance and store the psychological energy of sexual feeling to enhance creative performance. To store sexual energy for greater creative performance is rather like collecting psychological pleasantries as if they were sugar packets full of gunpowder. When appropriate, when you're ready, you can combine them all and make the most amazing fire-cracker you've ever seen.

If you've never done this before, you may not follow what I've just said. This is a specific method I use. (FYI: This is my six-teenth book created using this method, although most of the others were published pseudonymously.) I imagine I have a cobalt blue Mason jar with a lid. Each spark of sexual energy I manage to capture is a firefly I put into the jar. The fireflies of energy live happily in the jar. When I am ready to be creative (or more accurately, when I am on deadline!), I open the jar and the joyous, grateful fireflies flurry into the universe and bring me back bits of universal intelligence as parting gifts before they fly away. I weave these into a book.

In her profound book *The Artist's Way*, Julia Cameron writes about journaling. In her words, you should write "morning pages"—stream of consciousness thoughts journaled upon awak-ening. Perhaps she's aware that part of what you capture first thing in the morning are random bits of sexual energy tossed with a potpourri of other things. I suggest further that writing or consciously journaling your sexuality can be like Viagra to your creative energy.

Shelly, an artist friend, left this week for a six-month stay in Ireland. She leaves behind her husband, two dogs and a house. Six months of celibacy will be an interesting time for this late-forties woman to invest her energy in her art, her creativity and coming to know herself better.

Will she miss her husband? I'm sure she will, but artists have been known to take long periods of celibacy to pour their crea-tive energy into their artwork. Artists of all types learn to trans-mute their sexual energy into creativity.

Victoria, a writer you read about earlier, told me that the primary way she rechannels her sexual energy is into her creativity. "When I apply the intensity of focus to my work, it brightens what I am writing," she said.

Women report that celibacy enhances their creativity in all aspects of their lives. It enhances their attention to their careers, homes, health and children. All these areas require focus and energy, and when you feel like you are doing well in one area, it boosts your self-confidence and makes you more appealing to new friends and new experiences.

Back to Love

A relationship only represents a small portion of a person's life. I want the whole enchilada. I want to wake up each morning in love with myself, with my life and with the people in it. How do we make that happen on a regular basis? We focus our intentions on what we wish to achieve in any aspect of our lives with a sexual energy chaser.

As women, the concept of using our sexual energy—or even having it—is a relatively new idea. So is planning to achieve great things. It's time we put an end to thinking of ourselves secretly as still unworthy or incapable. It's time we stopped feeding ourselves the Cinderella myth promulgated in books with titles like *How to Marry a Rich Man* and *How to Make a Man Fall in Love with You*. It's time we stopped allowing ourselves to be stereotyped as being from the planet Venus, and it is way beyond time we finally say to men, "Look, cave or no cave, this Mars behavior is infantile and counterproductive." Screw the "real moments," girls. Let's get out there and make life happen!

We are on the crest of a new era in male-female relations. Having gone through millennia of oppression we are at last in a place where we can step out onto the platform of power and safely claim a place for ourselves, too. We can finally create a masterpiece with both colors—the male and the female. We can choose to create, if nothing else, harmony between the sexes. We fought the good fight for our independence and we won, but while both genders exist on this planet, it is wise to assume that we are victors and losers in our own war. Therefore, we are now also in position to negotiate our own peace treaty with men.

One of the most interesting things a life of celibacy provides is a chance to get to know yourself and the people in your life in a way you have never done before. If you always wanted to pick up a hobby, although that sounds trite until you've done it, you have a real chance to do it when you are celibate. If you are a single parent and worry about not spending enough time with your kids or not having enough time for yourself, becoming a BAV will give time to include that in your life. If you want to build your empire, here's your big chance.

The useless-sock syndrome is all in our heads, ladies. The idea that we need a man to function went out with wearing aprons to bake cookies. The reality of our lives today is that we are capable of creating whatever we want in our lives, and the only way to create anything is to put positive attention on it for sufficient duration, as well as to have the basic skills and tools necessary to complete the task.

Becoming a BAV will give you the most critical skills you need to grow yourself into the next stage of your existence. It will give you the opportunity to grow *yourself*. No one else has the power to attract terrific men into your life, to create wealth or a

dynamic career for yourself, or a fit body or to have a great relationship with your kids. No one else gets to decide if you even
become a mother. The power to control our lives is ours alone,
in a way that was not available to our grandmothers. We have the
chance, if we will only use it, to make radical changes in any
areas of our lives that are not working for us. Will you accept the
challenge of living in your greatness?

SEVEN

Health, Wealth, Happiness and Great Sex

*There are a number of
mechanical devices which increase
sexual arousal, particularly in
women. Chief among them is
the Mercedes-Benz 380SL
convertible.*

P. J. O'ROURKE

There are as many reasons for becoming a born-again virgin as there are women who make the choice. Each of us has our own reasons, our own intended benefits. As you know from the list in chapter 1, there are also some real, practical and universal benefits to becoming a BAV. There's also the list of goals you wrote out in chapter sex.

One of the primary benefits women experience when reclaiming their sexual natures appears to be the accompanying sense of self-love and self-esteem. Self-love is critical before we can love others, and reclaiming our sexuality is for some women a way of increasing their own sense of self-control and self-respect. Many of the women I interviewed reported feelings of greater control over their hormones, their dating life, their futures, their moods and attitudes.

Celibacy can have a transformational effect on women. It strengthens our lives, replenishes our emotional reserves and makes us better able to form healthy connections of every type with others. While celibate, women have found more time to spend with their kids, to get back into hobbies or to increase their career focus and create a lot more income. In every case, no matter the extent of virginity they chose, the choice led them to feel more aware and empowered and informed about the roles their bodies play in the culture.

One of the remarkable benefits and transcendent qualities for women so inclined is the development of purer attitudes of service and dedication to loftier goals. Some women find themselves coming into alignment with higher spiritual values as a result of their decision not to have sex. They experience a sense of mission and a direction leading to fulfillment of their lives' purposes and ultimate goals.

When I asked Susie to meet me to discuss her sexuality, she was eager. In the time I'd known her since her major breakup, she had totally transformed herself. Although she is quite pretty and sophisticated, in the beginning she had almost no confidence. Her job search was going poorly, she was using the revolving-door method of dating and she seemed bitter about it all. Now she is vibrant, well-employed in her chosen field, and seems confident and happy. I asked her about the changes.

"It wasn't like I couldn't say no before to guys. I wasn't a nympho or anything like that. It's just that since Ted and I broke up, I realized I was using sex to kind of blunt the pain. Like an escape or a drug or something," Susie explained. She pushed her long chestnut brown hair back over her shoulder and smiled. "And then one day I just said, 'That's it! I've had enough of this!' I was dating a guy at the time, and he'd just gone home. I realized that I didn't love him, I wasn't even really sure if I liked him. We'd done it on our second date and after that it was just kind of expected."

Susie realized that her sexuality was a tool she was using to not deal with the realities of her relationships, and she simply stopped having sex five months ago. "My whole outlook changed," she said. "Before I used to panic if I didn't have a date for the weekend and wonder how I could possibly get through a week without sex. Now I find my life has taken on a whole new energy level."

Susie said, "I spend more time taking care of myself. I dress nicely because I want to dress nicely—not because I want to attract anybody. I spend more time with other women and more time doing things that are fun and important to me. Besides, if I go out with a guy I like, to see what kind of person he is, it's not like I'm going to be better at deciding if he's right for me if I sleep with him."

Sex appeal is 50 percent what you've got—
and 50 percent what people think you've got.

SOPHIA LOREN, INTERNATIONAL SCREEN STAR

She told me her life has changed in lots of other ways, too. Her newfound confidence and self-esteem, which are the most commonly reported results of celibacy, have given her the confidence to apply for jobs she previously would have been too nervous and self-effacing to attempt. Now she moves with confidence, around men and around women.

Women who choose to become born-again virgins commonly talk about their energy being higher and more positive. It seems that this comes from stopping the flow of energy it takes to chase and be chased. If you think about how much time we spend as single females, preening and pining for the other sex, you start to realize the profound effect celibacy can have on a woman's life, not to mention her free time.

In my own experience as a single mom, I used to date a lot when my ex had visitation. I found myself playing all weekend and then chatting with the guy on the phone during the week. When I stopped being sexual, I found I had a whole lot more time with and emotional space for my daughter. I was able to focus much more calmly and completely on her and her needs and her character development, as opposed to dividing my time between her and a guy.

Another surprise I found was that celibacy strengthened my friendships with men and women. The guy friends knew that sex wasn't an issue, so the ones who had maintained that expectation drifted off. The women friends who are focused on bagging the nearest male, preferably for marriage, also floated away, or at least they stopped talking to me incessantly about their struggles with men. Several of them have even become "converts" to BAV.

I found without talking about men, sex, dating, where to find men and all those related topics, I was able to have interesting, fulfilling, absorbing discussions on a variety of topics. When you haven't been out partying the night before in the vain hope you'll meet someone, it's much more fun to wake up the next morning and go out to a museum or take care of yourself in a nice, refreshing way. I really value my free, clear-thinking time.

Liz laughed as she slipped a sequined dress over her head. A talented actress, she is always laughing and bubbly. Liz is a born-again virgin who still goes out to her favorite nightclubs and cocktail parties and lives in a whirl of Beverly Hills social life, but she decided not to sleep with anyone until the time was right for her. We were standing in the middle of her living room, waiting to go out to dinner together at a nightclub. She was late getting dressed, as usual. "I'd *never* give up *the chase!*" she announced. "That's the fun of it! It's just the getting caught part that takes all the time and makes me feel tired and frustrated."

Liz has been divorced for nine years and is now in her early fifties. Her kids are grown and out of the house, and last year she made the decision to abstain. She told me her therapist suggested it when she broke up with her boyfriend. Liz said, "I was running around and going out with guys without thinking first. I'd see someone cute and I'd feel lonely and so I'd say yes. That's how I started dating Jimmy."

When Jimmy met Liz at a swanky bar, they became friends and fast lovers. Jimmy moved in, ate Liz's food, told her about his yacht and laid around watching her television while she went to work being *on* television. He was down on his luck, he told her when she suggested he could help pay some of the rent since he had been living there for months. He felt like helping out financially or physically by repairing a few things would be too much of a commitment for him at the time, so he moved back onto his "yacht," which turned out to be little more than a dinghy. Liz was furious and hurt and felt stupid. It was the last straw.

She realized she was making some bad choices in her life, choices made out of loneliness, fear of aging and weakness—not out of power. So she stopped. As a BAV, she now goes out to the same parties and flirts just as shamelessly with men. She loves the energy, and they love her. Now, though, when they make a move, she just tells them, "Nope. I don't get involved with men I don't know very well yet." She reports, "I'm making more money now and am at a higher level in my career than I could have ever imagined when I got divorced!" She has no intention of staying single, and she'll tell you today she believes her chances of remarrying have gone up dramatically since she began "holding out." She values herself at a higher level, and men follow suit.

In a few cases, the men react in disbelief. Other times, they promptly offer to take her to dinner, the theater or a host of other places. Other times they walk away, looking for easier prey. Liz still walks away every time knowing she's the one in charge and knowing she can change her mind at any time for the right man and the right reasons.

Liz attracts quite a number of men interested in her perky personality, her warm compassionate side and her petite but buxom body. She feels empowered by realizing that she makes all the choices when it comes to when, how and if she expresses her sexuality while dating. "It's exhilarating," she said. "It's made me so much more focused in every area of my life. Instead of wondering if this one would work out or if that one would call me, I now spend my time working on me, on my life, on my career." She's seen a resurgence in her career since her decision—even doing a six-night stint on the stage in Vegas.

One woman told me that making such conscious choices is like the high runners get when they break through exhaustion: It's pure air, it's clear, and you can see yourself and your behavior and your life and everyone else from a whole new perspective—and perspective is what it's all about for many BAVs. It's about being able to step back from the frenzy of man hunting and dating and wondering if you have condoms in stock. It's about being able to get a new perspective on an old relationship or to empower yourself to leave your current one.

"I stayed because I didn't know what would be on the other side," Sandy told me. "I stayed with Ron far too long because I was afraid that if I went 'out there' into the dating world, I would not be able to deal with the loneliness and the new sex partners and trying to decide who I wanted to be with or find someone I could even stand. I figured Ron's problems weren't that bad, and I guess I really just feared the unknown."

Sandy looked down at her short, clean nails. Her kids were asleep in the other room. Leaving her bad marriage had taken a lot of courage, but she was finding the strength to build a new life. Sitting on her couch, cradling a cup of peppermint tea, she told me, "In the beginning, I thought I'd probably be the type to just take the next guy who offered." She laughed. "I mean, I didn't think I was exactly a hot commodity with three kids. But when I found the courage to be okay with who I am and where I'm at in my life, and to take a breather between my marriage ending and my dating life, I found I had strengths I didn't even know I had!" It has been a year and a half, and although she dated one guy for a few months in the beginning, when that didn't work out, she took some time for herself.

One of the more surprising things Sandy told me about herself, and that I also found to be true after my divorce, was a renewed interest in hobbies. I'm talking about "free time," that rarity for single mothers. Sandy told me that after her kids are in bed, she pulls out her watercolor paints and works on her art. It's something she gave up when she dropped out of college art classes to have her first kid. "It's amazing the joy it gives me!" she said. "I'd forgotten all about how much I love it. I'd always thought, 'Well, when the kids are older,' but now I find myself being a better, more peaceful mother because I am also taking time to do something I love—okay, something I love a bit more than dishes and housework," she finished with a laugh.

"I have a real sense of calm about it all," she told me. "It's like I am not going to jump into another relationship just because I'd like some help with the kids. They'll be gone someday, and I will have to live with myself and whatever guy I am married to then. For me, being celibate helps me wait without jumping back in too fast."

A common thread of relief in the divorced women I spoke with was a chance to reevaluate their needs and desires for a man. Pam, a twenty-something newcomer to celibacy with plenty of experience on the dating trail, harbors some bitterness toward men. "What do you call that useless piece of skin on the end of a penis?" she asked me acerbically. "A foreskin?" I replied, sure for some reason this wouldn't be the right answer. "No, a man!" It was this bitterness and sarcasm—the result of being sexual and hurt since she was thirteen—that had forced her to take a good long look at her life and goals. Now she's taking time before she gets involved again to decide what she wants, how she wants to be treated and what a good life would look like to her. She also says it's much easier not to have a guy in your apartment when you get home from work. She's taking time to heal.

> *Marriage is a great institution.*
> *But I'm not ready for an institution.*
>
> MAE WEST, ACTRESS, WRITER

Especially for women who are just leaving long-term relationships, the lack of regular, predictable sex can be alarming. Yet it is probably these very women who need to take a break the most. As we grieve the loss of relationships—even ones we wanted out of—we empower ourselves by sifting through the rubble. In these pieces of our past, we can find bits of broken memories and tinges of forgotten pain, and by reviewing and analyzing these life fragments, we can make better choices next time. "Those who do not learn from the mistakes of history are destined to repeat them" (source unknown).

"Once you know what you really want, not what you see on TV that looks good, you really feel like you can get it if you don't settle. I believe we all get what we settle for," Pam said triumphantly. "I don't know how long it will last, but being a— what do you call it?—born-again virgin has really changed my life and given me a resting spot."

How do you really *know* if being a BAV for a while—or for a lifetime—is good for you? First of all, it's not like breast enhancement surgery! It isn't permanent, doesn't hurt and doesn't cost anything. It's like a temporary tattoo—you can wear it, try it out, see how it feels. You can see if it changes the way you feel about yourself and the way others respond to you. If you take it off and want to go back, you can. If you decide to make it part of your permanent image, you can do that, too.

EIGHT

Sex, Religion and Spirituality

He that on Earth
from Birth to Death observes
Chastity, for him there is nothing
beyond reach, know this,
O Herdsmen of men.

THE *VEDAS*

The Bible relates the story of a harlot who was caught in the act with a man. According to some sources, he was a married man of note in the town. (You will note his behavior is not condemned within the Bible's highly patriarchal society.) The officials in the town, seeking to make

Christ judge another harshly and thus divert part of his loyal following, brought the ashamed woman to him. Can you imagine how she must have felt?

Christ observed the situation and made the famous statement "Let him who be innocent cast the first stone." He invited the officials to stone her on the spot, as was appropriate under the law. Before they could do so, he quietly stooped down and wrote a list of the townspeople's sins in the dust. No one threw a stone. In fact, they slipped away guiltily and the woman was spared. Christ sent her off with the admonition to "Go and sin no more." He believed she could change in an *instant*. So can you.

I believe the point of that story is that at any given moment each of us may choose to forgive ourselves for any regrets of our past. We are all one moment, one decision away from being as pure and white as virgins, if that is the choice we would like to make. Our baggage is so often a vast array of ugly plastic luggage crammed full of "If only I" and "I should have" and "I wish I hadn't." Being a BAV gives you the opportunity to put all that down and walk away from it. You can start over with a new life, an empty suitcase. You get to go forward, you get to pass Go and collect $200, you get another chance. Take it!

What sort of women can we become if we hold our sexual energy—which is our essential and most powerful life energy—as sacred to ourselves? What power can we wield when we move onto a higher plane of spiritual existence in this life through the choice of abstinence? What service can we render as individuals and as women when we are unburdened by the raging hormones that drive us today?

The summary benefits of temporary or permanent celibacy for most women seem to be a greater sense of self-love and self-esteem. As we are told over and over by psychologists, before we can really love another we must first learn to really love ourselves.

Yet we observe throughout history that large groups of women, particularly nuns, chose to refrain from sexual contact in order to enter into a time of meditation and spiritual growth. From the Hindu *Bhagavad Gita* to the Christian Bible, chastity and restraint and even releasing yourself entirely from bondage to human sexuality are encouraged as methods of increasing spiritual understanding and inviting purity into your life.

I perceive in my studies that women who act with love toward humankind—Helen Keller, Mother Teresa, Florence Nightingale and millions of others—are the women who have developed within themselves the greatest capacity for self-love. They are so full of love and acceptance of themselves that they naturally love and accept and help others. Their lives, while not always ideal, represent for many women a higher level of service that perhaps remains elusive in our own lives. The Bible says, "Love your neighbor *as yourself*," and this precept is found as well in all other great spiritual traditions.

On a more personal scale—relationships with your employees, your coworkers, your children, your extended family—what effect would truly and deeply loving and revering yourself have on your relationships with them? Could the tool of celibacy be used for a while or for a lifetime to help you achieve your goals in this world?

Each woman must choose for herself the path that she will follow. The seeds she sows today will yield the harvest she will reap in the future. If you desire the fruits shared by women in this book, becoming a born-again virgin just might be right for you.

For the Love of God

Since the dawn of time, men and women who wanted to dedicate themselves to God renounced their physical desires and became priests, monks and nuns. They did this so time that might have been spent raising a family and catering to a mate could be diverted to religious study and service to God. As one former novitiate (an about-to-be-nun) told me, "Sexuality is sublimated. You can mow the grass because it needs to be mowed, or you can mow it to the glory of God. It's your perspective. Not being sexual is sanctifying myself for the glory of God—the lesser issue of sensual gratification doesn't even enter into the matter."

Most religious communities and belief systems around the world honor sex as holy union, a sacrament or sacred, even if they do not permit their clergy to be sexual. They almost universally teach respect for the opposite gender, reverence for a Higher Power and sexuality as the spark that brings the gift of life. Teaching love for the other can never be wrong, and, in the instance of celibacy, it permits time to develop feelings of affection, kindness, openness and sharing with another that may never otherwise happen in our modern culture.

Long ago, lay people marveled at those so dedicated to God that they would voluntarily give up sex in order to serve the Lord and their community. Today we wonder if maybe those crotchety old nuns don't just need to get laid. We wonder if modern monks, priests, nuns and others who are celibate in traditional religious orders fantasize about sex or if they cheat on their vows. Probably some do, but in my interviews with several, their insider perspective is that the majority of their peers and they themselves are consciously diverting sexual gratification for nobler, loftier goals.

In *The New Celibacy,* Gabrielle Brown states, "Unlike hunger, thirst and the craving for intimacy—which are the real needs— physical sexual gratification is far less necessary than imagined." It's the emotional intimacy that most of us desire, and for some people, living in a community of like-minded believers is exactly the tranquility and intimacy they need. As one woman said, "Celibacy gives me the opportunity to take a broader look at my life. I see others' behaviors and I see my own much more clearly from this perspective."

In her best-selling book *The Cloister Walk,* author Kathleen Norris describes her experience of entering a convent for a while to pursue religious studies. She is married when she makes the choice but feels the urge to listen to a higher calling. She speaks also of hoping the decision will help her think through her relationship with her husband and with her God and that perhaps she will leave the convent with a greater sense of commitment to her marriage. She immerses herself in ritual and duty and finds it transcends the physical and cracks open new light like the first rays of dawn on the ocean.

One of the many interesting observations Norris makes in her book is her take on a work by Saint Benedict called *The Rule of the Master.* She quotes him as writing, "Whoever needs less should thank God and not be distressed. Whoever needs more should feel humble because of his weakness, not self-important because of the kindness shown him. In this way, all the members will be at peace."

How Much Sex Do You Need?

Peace is something most people seek in this crazy world. What would be the outcome of applying the concept of needing less being a blessing to our sexuality, instead of worrying that we are not in a relationship, or having enough sex, or getting as much as someone else? With our cultural emphasis on an individual's worth being not about who we are but who we are with, surely those who feel the call to celibacy for any reason could count themselves grateful. What blessings could come from the gift of freedom from sexuality?

> *The gift of celibacy is, in reality,*
> *the call to be a "seer."*
>
> JOSEPH WADE, PRIEST

Norris comments that "While Benedict respected the individual, he recognized that the purpose of individual growth is to share with others"—to share with others from the abundance of who we are: our love, our goodness, our time.

Born in 480 A.D. in Italy, Saint Benedict was the founder of the monastic Benedictines and a major supporter of civilization in Christian Europe. He died on March 21, 547 A.D., in prayer before the altar. He was noted for his sanctity and this attracted others to follow him. His rule of life was very strict and summed up as "a life of sacrifice, prayer, simplicity, study, hard work and community living."

A charming nun I interviewed told me, "The monastic order flourished because it fulfilled people's need for challenges. People aren't always looking for an easy life. People are truly looking for a challenge, to make sacrifices, to try to live the harder things. A person can choose to make better decisions and live a purer life. I think even today people have too much and now they are willing to sacrifice. They want to sacrifice for something. They see one of the benefits of sacrifice is a happy life. People who have less and are always ready to give more are happier and stronger and better people."

If you believe a deity created you, isn't it logical that you have within you the equipment for listening to the voice of the heavens? When the voice inside you is crying out for space, for an alteration of your sexual behavior, isn't it only to your own detriment not to listen? Who is to say you weren't led to consider the issue of celibacy or even led to read this book at this exact moment in your life?

You know that feeling when you are embroiled in a bad relationship and everything seems to be getting worse and worse? Your mind is screaming out for some "think time" but creating that in our whirlwind lives is nearly impossible. Wouldn't it be nice to call a sexual truce, to withhold sex without feeling guilty, while you take time to sort out the relationship?

In traditional Judeo-Christian doctrine, God provides times of respite from sexuality even for people who are married. The Jews believe in Niddah, which is a state of separating the self from sexuality during menstruation. A traditional Jewish woman today would separate herself from her husband from the onset of menstruation for ten to fourteen days, or until there is no more blood or discharge of any kind. The woman then takes a ritual bath, immersing herself in a Mikvah, which is natural water, like the ocean or rainwater. Then she can resume sexual relations with her husband.

During Niddah, a woman has to communicate with her husband without touching him physically in any way. For instance, if a traditional woman is cooking dinner, she wouldn't hand the plate to her husband, she would set it down and let him pick it up himself, lest their hands brush against one another's and cause him to be aroused. This abstinence enhances the other aspects of a relationship.

I only wish brushing his wife's hand had that effect on most men. It is incumbent upon the man to respect his wife's need for privacy during that time. It's about respecting a woman's right to some time for herself. It's not a time of uncleanness but rather a time of respecting all aspects of life. It is a time to give her space to deal with her womanhood.

In Ethiopia some communities have special houses for menstruating women to go to. They can have their backs rubbed, have other people make food for them, escape from the routine of their lives for a while. Their husbands honor this respite for their wives. It sounds to me like these Ethiopian women are given a chance to celebrate life and reflect on who they are in a special way during their bleeding time.

In traditional Christianity, women are also provided with a time of separation during menstruation. Women also are told to celebrate sexual union and not to withhold sexual availability, either partner from the other, at any other time.

When I was a newlywed still making love like a rabbit, I couldn't imagine anything more inconvenient than having to refrain from sex during my period, but for religious reasons, we did abstain. This probably made a lot of sense in ancient times when showers and bathtubs were not common, but it didn't seem to make sense in this day and age. Years of married life went by. Two kids and a job and plenty of responsibilities later, I suddenly found myself grateful for my period, grateful for a week of no sex. It gave my husband and me time to talk about our relationship, to make sure we were happy and not harboring grudges. Slowly, I came to believe that it was a blessing and not a curse to have a week off every month. It also made us more passionate when we did resume sexual relations—both emotionally and physically. This was certainly temporary celibacy even while sleeping beside my sexual companion.

Whatever religious belief you subscribe to, or are thinking of subscribing to, celibacy can help you focus on the things that really matter. Whether it is following ancient laws about sexual intercourse that makes you feel connected with a Higher Power or having energy to go to synagogue on Saturday morning since you didn't screw anyone you met Friday night, abstinence can move you closer to your Creator.

Many believe that the expanded viewpoint provided by celibacy can help us look at our lives from a higher perspective, to see what contribution we are making. If you believe that you can attract the vibrations of your soul mate through meditation, or if you believe that by earnest prayer God will send that person to you, you are spending time focusing on what you want to get for yourself. You are directing valuable life energy into an outcome. The Bible says, "Choose the path" and "God will direct your steps." If you are so focused on finding a mate, perhaps even trying to use church as a place to find the right mate, you are taking your focus off greater spiritual values such as giving. Perhaps including giving in your desire to get a relationship would be wise.

Giving is the bottom line of every religion, belief and dogma, and truly honoring yourself and your sexuality through abstinence until marriage is a truly spiritual pursuit when it gives you time to teach Sunday school, to pray or meditate for someone who is ill, or to contribute money or other life resources to those in need. In other words, you can choose to direct your energy toward giving, loving one another and coming into harmony with Creation/Creator, or you can focus all your strength on finding a mate or a sexual partner. Which seems more spiritually minded to you? Which one evidences greater trust in the forces you believe in?

The true foundation of every religious group and spiritual practice is to give unto others, love one another and learn to more fully love oneself. I believe our physical bodies temporarily offer abode for the soul we remain lifetime after lifetime. Even the Bible calls our bodies the "Temple of the Soul." How much reverence is due to this temple in which we now live? Let's learn to live in the light of that knowledge by treating ourselves as the temple we are for our souls.

NINE

Becoming a Born-Again Virgin

I was on a date recently and the guy took me horseback riding. That was kind of fun, until we ran out of quarters.

SUSIE LOUCKE

So you think you're ready to take the big step and actually commit to becoming a born-again virgin? Great! Now what happens? Do you rush out and buy a chastity belt? (What in the heck *is* a chastity belt, anyway?)

The easiest way to be sure you're ready to become celibate for the rest of this week, this month, this year, this decade or this lifetime is to decide if it feels like the right choice to you, if it feels right and natural. That is not the same as being celibate by default, which means you want sex but you can't find any.

Does moving into celibacy feel like the right decision for you right now? (You don't have to decide on the duration.) This is not a test, but whatever you do, do what is right for you. If you find yourself going nuts sexually in forty-eight hours after making the choice, it's possible you're not ready. It's your body. It's your *right to choose.*

The women I talked to inducted themselves into the BAV sisterhood in different ways. For many, they simply took stock of their lives and stopped having sex with anyone who didn't meet their criteria. Some, like Allison (see Introduction), announced it frequently. I'm a diary person, so I wrote it in my diary in big letters, along with the date and time I made the decision. I removed all the preceding pages in my three-ring binder that were filled with ideas and notes about men I had dated and began fresh with new pages. One friend who liked the idea wrote herself Post-it notes and put them all over her apartment.

Another woman took becoming a BAV especially seriously. She bought four purple candles and picked some flowers. She wrote on slips of paper the names of the men she believes have caused her pain. She also wrote down her goal, like a mantra, on another sheet: "I want a fantastic relationship with a great man." One evening, she sat down, lit the candles and slowly burned the names, repeating the mantra as the names burned up. For what it's worth, she's married now and seems really happy.

You will know celibacy could work for you if after having sex you feel odd, sad, disconnected, weird or out of control. You know celibacy is working for you when you begin to feel better about your life. Usually, a celibate person will experience fewer sexual fantasies and urges as time passes, which is not to say such feelings cannot be stirred up again—quickly—but rather that the drive to be sexual gently takes a back seat while other values and needs come to the front.

I am not suggesting you stop being a sexual being. We are born with gender, so we cannot help but have sexual feelings. I am suggesting you can harness that energy in something akin to the Jewish practice of Niddah, the experience of being a wonderfully sexual being, fully capable of being sexual, and yet choosing to refrain within certain parameters. Niddah is a time of respecting oneself and the loveliness of sexuality when one is with one's chosen partner.

Does sexual intention wane? Will you stop lusting right away, as soon as you become a BAV? The camps are divided on this topic. Some women and men with whom I have spoken and some books I have read reported celibacy is *not* a mental decision, that it is a natural state that creeps upon one slowly. You suddenly realize you have no feelings of desire.

Others state that celibacy is a physical experience and that only people with a low sex drive can become celibate. For example, they say, nuns never think about it much, never do it, so it's no big loss for them. That's hard for me to believe. Nuns are human. The nuns I asked said that they had thought about it but that after a while other interests seemed so much more meaningful. They reminded me of the concept of sublimation—the use of the body for a higher purpose, for the glory of God.

Other people state, as I believe, that celibacy is by all means a mental decision, just like the judgment whether or not it was "good sex" is largely mental. Celibacy is definitely a decision to adopt for a time or a lifetime to help you sort through, heal, readjust or realign your life, goals and priorities.

Whatever the reason, different kinds of experiences occur for the newly celibate person. Some people experience no physical cravings at all. They simply make a mental and physical decision not to be sexual until further notice and begin living that way. For others, desire ebbs and flows. Some women report that during ovulation they begin checking out everything male, whether they do anything about it or not.

I asked Gloria (a BAV) about it, and she told me when she left her marriage, "I missed the frequency of sexual encounters. We were sexual right up until the end, twice a week. Suddenly, there wasn't anything. Here it is, three years later, and I don't even remember what regular sex was like. I don't think about it or wish for it. If I did, I'd remarry."

The difference between abstinence and celibacy is masturbation. Some women who are celibate are actually quite sexual, just not with a partner. They indulge in fantasies about sex while stimulating themselves. This type of sex for one usually decreases in someone who is truly assuming celibacy because there is no actual physical need associated with sexual behavior. Unlike our need for water, food and shelter, you don't need sex to live, and after a while, you may not care about self-pleasuring. You may be in such a peaceful state that you are content to grow yourself and wait to see what happens, or you may get so clever at redirecting sexual energy toward your goals or creativity that it becomes automatic.

For most women, sexual desire recedes gradually over a few months. One stops thinking about it, and there is a whole new sense of peace and purpose. Then, if someone worthy of you actually catches your sexual attention, your sexual nature blossoms again like a cactus in the desert after a rain. It's not like we lose our ability to be sensual or sexual.

Around the early 1900s, the idea came to Western medicine that *not* using one's sexual organs would cause them to waste away. Eventually, various doctors in sexually repressed Victorian England and the United States decided that sexual organs *should* be used. Masturbation was encouraged by these people. Others contested that it was indecent. Young boys were told they'd go blind or grow fur on the palms of their hands if they masturbated. Nice little girls were scolded if they touched themselves when they took off their diapers. Those who were against masturbation believed that "wasting" sperm (as if there weren't enough!) used up a man's life energy because a man's energy lives within his sperm. If that were true, conserving it would be wise, as it would prolong a man's life and energy.

This idea was stolen, of course, from the Eastern cultures where for thousands of years men had been cumming without ejaculation. Many cultures, including Buddhists, believe that sperm and life energy of the male can be wasted by ejaculation.

In the Tao—written like the Bible by men for a select group of men who were the only ones taught to read at that time—men are encouraged not to reach orgasm. It was thought that ejaculation cost a man a tiny speck of his life energy because he was planting that speck of himself in a woman's body. There is the theory that one reason women live longer is because they gather up all this life seed.

I find these opinions excessively patriarchal in their viewpoint. Where is the tradition of a woman's life energy being

wasted by servicing men's needs? Could it stand to reason that
men have overlooked us? Could it be possible that women also
lose energy or life force when they climax sexually? Ask yourself
this: Do you feel rejuvenated after sex or debilitated? The
answer will vary from woman to woman, in my casual research,
and it will also vary from climax to climax. The Oriental theory
is apparently that we take life energy from the man, which
accounts for why we live longer. (If that were true, nuns would
always die first!)

It may be true that it is (also) *our* life energy expended in the
sex act because, as more emotional beings, very few women can
honestly say that sex does not affect their feelings about a man.
Our feelings are part of our lives because they are a representa-
tion of our souls. So it is we who are laying a piece of our life
down on the mattress every time. If that piece is given to a man,
and then to another, and then yet another, we dissipate our life
essence, our own emotional life energy, by scattering pieces of
ourselves over a wide number of partners.

Based on that theory, the assumption could be made that the
remedy for scattered emotional energy is abstinence. Perhaps it is
similar to the way that some of the lung tissue damaged by smoking regenerates a bit more every day a smoker doesn't light up. It
could be postulated that every man you pass up, every fleeting
sexual encounter you pass up because you already know it would
be wrong for you repairs a tiny bit of what you have lost in your
heart so far. It's possible. It is even logical based on this model.

I don't have and, in all the materials I have read, cannot find
the answer to this question of whether or not women lose or gain
energy/life force or even whether it is irrelevant. Perhaps no male
doctor has cared enough to ask. Perhaps women were so long a

commodity that no civilization one thousand years ago thought much about it.

Let's be the first women to think this through. Consider the following questions.

[If you want to be part of my empirical research on this interesting subject, please email me (*www.bornagainvirgins.com*) or write me c/o Health Communications, Inc., with your answers to the following questions and your observations on the same.]

1. Do you take, give or remain neutral regarding life force/energy during sex?

2. Do you feel more energized or less energized after you climax. Is it always one way rather than the other? If so, which way is it for you?

3. Is your sexual response the same if he wears a condom (in which case you would not physically receive the sperm)?

4. Is your sexual response the same if he has had a vasectomy (in which case the sperm would be "deactivated")?

I will speculate a bit about what your answers might indicate: If he wears a condom and you report you feel more energized, it could mean (in true Chinese fashion) that the invisible energy/life force has been transferred into your body—directly into your chakra. (Sorry to mix ideologies!) If he wears a condom and you feel less energized and you feel more energized without condoms, it could mean that the energy/life spark is, literally, in the physical sperm itself. If you never feel energized with your lover who has a vasectomy, it could mean that the life spark is removed when the viability of the sperm is removed, which also could mean that men who have vasectomies should be healthier or live longer. If you always feel energized by your lover and he has a vasectomy, it could again mean that the life spark is really something energetic.

I will publish the results after I receive at least three hundred responses, either in another book or on the Internet of the BAVs website. It will be interesting if someday a real scientist evaluates if we do or do not "suck the life" out of men and if the idea of "nonejaculative male orgasm" really does prolong male life or improve men's health. In any case, whether or not we are "sucking" energy from men or they are giving or taking it from us has little to do with the reasons women become celibate.

Okay, enough research. I'm looking forward to hearing your responses. Who knows? We could be conducting major research here that changes forever the way people look at their sexuality.

The Ins and Outs of Celibacy

Rebecca told me, "It's not sex I miss. That's easy to live without. It's even easy to, as you said, redirect. What I miss and don't get is touching and cuddling stuff. I miss affection. I grew up in a touchy-feely sort of family. I live fifteen hundred miles away from them now. I miss touching more than sex."

Where do people in our modern society get enough touching? Who nurtures adults? Who nurtures, touches and cuddles you?

Where do you get enough touching, holding, cuddling? Women report that they often trade sex for nurturing and touching, especially in our "keep your hands to yourself" culture. How do single celibate women find enough tactile interaction with other human beings?

I discussed this topic with Donna Marie Williams, author of *Sensual Celibacy* (which is a great book). Donna believes celibate women simply *must* dedicate time to other sensual delights because it's a very real need.

First, if you think about it, we're not that far from monkeys genetically. Monkeys spend their all of their days touching, picking at, playing with and rolling around with other monkeys. When we were a more agrarian society, most parents and children slept in the same one-room house and had regular physical contact, despite what we saw on *Little House on the Prairie*. Touching one another has been common all along our evolutionary trail until now.

Therefore, it is incredibly important that you find ways to interact physically with other human beings during the time you are celibate. Intimacy—sharing ideas and feelings, and touching others—are important ways we fill our need for belongingness and community.

In some cultures, it is wholly acceptable for women to hold hands, hug and kiss cheeks in public and in private. The issue has nothing to do with sexual preference. This probably socially conditions certain groups of women to receive limited tactile stimulation from other than a mate.

For women who are single mothers, touching is less of an issue. With a kid clambering over your lap, crawling into your bed to avoid monsters at 3:00 A.M. or wanting to be carried in sleeping from the car, single moms give lots of touching, and the ones I informally surveyed said they are only rarely conscious of a lack of physical touching in their lives.

In our society, the vestiges of Puritanism remain to this day. Long ago, child-rearing practices encouraged parents to refrain as much as possible from holding or caressing their children, lest they become weak and insipid. In our land of pioneers, with high infant mortality rates and short life expectancies, this may have been a reasonable adaptation.

Further, married adults were shamed if they were being sexual without conception as a motive in the privacy of their own bedrooms during the time of the pilgrims all the way into the early 1900s. Sex was a no-no, something one did for the sake of procreation but never for fun. So what point could there possibly be in frustrating oneself by being physically affectionate—and never in public? What would the neighbors think? Think of the married couples on *The Dick Van Dyke Show*—they slept in separate beds their whole lives.

As far as we've come, we still haven't shaken off this don't-touch issue. If you've traveled to Europe or Asia, you know people in certain races will get right in your personal space. For an American or British person, this can be upsetting. Being jostled in the Orient is a highly uncomfortable feeling for people who have been socialized to maintain at least twelve inches of personal space in every direction at all times.

Even in our families, a chaste hug and quick dry kiss on the cheek are typical behavior, and many families do not go even that far. So where can we get the touching we all need?

In a long-ago study conducted on wartime orphans, nurses were instructed not to fondle, talk to or be nice to newborn babies. The nation conducting the study wanted to see what sort of people these infants would become if they were raised without any human interaction other than perfunctory activities such as diaper changing—no warmth, no love, no touching. The study never reached a conclusion—because all the babies died!

Meeting our very human need for touching and interaction is critically important for us to learn if we are going to be celibate and not sell out. So how does one do it?

My first and most valuable suggestion on the subject is to *get involved.* I know a place where people get even less touching than you but need it more. I know a place where the people are sweet, kind, loving and funny and would appreciate ten minutes a month of your time in a way no other person ever could. I know people who are imprisoned after a lifetime of touching other people and now touch almost no one, certainly not anyone who isn't helping them. The place: the local senior center right in your town.

These old folks would love nothing better than to hold your hand and tell you what a sweet, nice girl you are for thirty minutes while they regale you with stories of the good old days. It doesn't matter who you are, it doesn't matter how much money you have, it doesn't matter how much time you have to spend there. If you want something, you have to learn to give it first, and giving a few minutes a month to a senior center is one of the best ways I can think of to get touching and a sense of belonging and community. Whenever I enter such places, I am struck by two things: how loving these people are, however powerful and gruff they may have been forty years earlier, and how soon it will be that I am in their place wishing for a bright young face to drop by to say hi and hold my hand.

Other community services in your area offer you vast opportunities to get involved. There are literacy programs to teach, kids to tutor, homes to help build, Girl Scout troops to help out and Big Sister programs to get into. There are people out there who need to be touched by you way, way more than you need to be touched by them. The payoff is not only the hugs and warm fuzzies you'll get; it's also some really amazing warm memories and real honest acceptance.

Naturally, at 7:30 A.M. on Saturday night you aren't going to be hanging out at the senior center hoping to get hugged. So how do you nurture yourself when you're not involved in service? Here's a list compiled from women I asked "How do you nurture yourself/indulge your sensuality when you are alone?"

A hot bubble bath

A cup of tea and a romance novel

A massage

Work out at a gym

Stretch or do yoga

A weekend at a spa with a girlfriend

A manicure/pedicure

Great bed sheets

Build a fire and put on cozy sweats

Play wonderful music

Take a class in something tactile (sewing, stained glass, water polo)

Gardening

Hiking

Playing with pet(s)

Wearing luxurious undergarments

Day to day, though, how do you create touching and nurturing opportunities? Although it may feel unnatural at first, when you walk into work in the morning you can hug (or become) the most gregarious person in your office or the sweet old receptionist. You can smile and clasp people's hands with both of yours when you shake hands, looking straight in their eyes while you do it—it will make you feel amazingly connected and them amazingly warm.

You won't know until you try it who you can hug, touch or cry with, but you'll soon pick up clues if anything you do is too much for them. Somebody has to start societal changes. Why not you and me? I have a male friend who also lives alone. There is zero chance of us being sexual in the future, but when we greet one another, we hug—sometimes for a minute or two—just enjoying the proximity of another adult.

The issue about touching people is that most people are as starved for physical interaction as you are, even if they are in a relationship. Remember, our natural tendency as beings is to touch and hug one another. We were very physically interactive as kids. Adults don't lose that desire. They stifle it. By you taking the first steps, you can create "hugging partners" (without perhaps identifying them as such) all around you. You'd be surprised what an honest, open, nonsexual exchange of physical interaction can do to brighten your day.

All of these methods have a psychological benefit as well as a physical one. Remember Maslow's sense of belongingness and community? You will feel more involved and closer to the people around you when you toss off this silly cultural moray of twelve inches of distance at all times and start opening up to being warm to people.

Reach Out and Touch Someone

We spend our days living from moment to moment, hand to mouth in the truest sense. We live as if the next item on our to-do list really is critical to our happiness, as if it really mattered in the overall scheme of things. How rarely we are able to step back from our self-imposed frenetic pace and see the world as it is— existing with and without us simultaneously, for we are in the world but we are not the world. Our component may be vital or it may not, but whether or not the dishes are washed or the house is dusted pales in comparison to whether or not we are fulfilling our life purpose in this instant.

Have you noticed in yourself, as I have in myself, the "I'll get to that when I am done with this" syndrome? Have you noticed that you procrastinate naturally on the really important things you want to do with your life? Have you noticed that when it comes to thinking through where you are at this instant and where you are going, it's so easy to shove it under the rug of schedules and commitments and responsibilities?

How do we stop and step back from the pace we have created? Meditation is one way to do this. From the purview of conscious stopping we can make a small space in the thick screen of our lives and perhaps see through the veil to the reality of what we are, instead of what we do.

Prayer, meditation, solitude. These have been used from the dawn of humankind to achieve different states of consciousness. American Indians still use sweat lodges and vision quests, and monks still use meditation and fasting and chanting. Whatever the method, the wise among us have always realized a place exists for breathing space.

As a single mother, it seems my life is set up to prevent me from having extra time or space. Owning a home and a business also seems to wash out any semblance of free time. Yet I find that when I commit to myself—to my spiritual nature—to set aside even a brief amount of time to honor the other side of life, I can see further and more clearly.

I believe that human beings, left unchecked, will live their lives precisely as the birds or the wolves or the rabbits, by which I mean that we will spend our lives hunting for food and shelter. Maslow's Hierarchy of Needs certainly indicates that until the lower needs are fulfilled, we rarely take time to ponder the value of our existence. He speaks of self-actualization—living consciously—as being the highest goal of humanity.

Currently, it is popular to "evolve," to believe in past lives, to be an "old soul," to bandy about pseudospiritual phrases and speak of the Vedas and gurus and use other language of spiritual evolution. I believe this is good only insofar as it is sincere. Parroting the right words, reading the right books, attending the right lectures and getting the momentary high from sitting through an inspiring worship service are meaningless unless we can incorporate our higher consciousness into our daily lives.

So how do we actually "walk the talk"? How do we actually use all this newfound spirituality to improve the quality of our lives? It's all well and good to believe you've lived past lives, but what about paying for your kid's college education in this one? What about the problems you have with your boss or the fact that no matter what you ate yesterday you have to find another meal today to survive.

Incorporating our spirituality into our lives implies that we live at the very edge of this world we have created. It implies that we make our spirituality a priority in every moment of our lives. When you consider the fringes of all religious groups, there is a common denominator. Christ, Buddha, Krishna and all other enlightened beings who we are conscious of have expressed one common thing: love—love for self and love for others.

All religious groups have at their essence love for self and others. Some would even claim that the divine itself is love in perfection. Love is that invisible energy that has such capacity to change lives, unite people, ease discord and bond people together.

If love is divine energy in action, or even a piece of the "holy spirit" flowing through our bodies, how do we increase our measure? How do we gain more love in our lives? How do the lonely single people of the world, the lonely married people of the world, the all-alone people of the world get more love and therefore more divine power?

The answer is by giving it away. This simple principle is espoused in every religious and spiritual doctrine, yet few people actually attempt to practice it. In our me-first world, we find ourselves pushing and shoving, lying and manipulating, vying for position—and that's just on the freeway! We cry "Every man for himself!" and we clamor up the "ladder" of success, which perhaps implies stepping on colleagues to rise.

Oppression is rampant in the history of humans: subjugation, slavery, cruelty, bigotry against women, children, other races, other beliefs. Very few wise souls have stood out in this melee of pain. Very few have actually incorporated a doctrine of love into their lives. Yet those who have are those we revere as saintlike: Mother Teresa, Princess Diana, John the Baptist, Joan of Arc, Florence Nightingale, Gandhi and others. These are the mighty few who were able to wield the power of love toward others and create a better world for us all.

In each very different case, the individual's personal circumstances at the time he or she began to show love for others vary greatly. Some lived in poverty, some in opulence, so we can conclude that life circumstances are not an adequate determinant of our ability to love others. Some came from broken homes, others from happy families. Some were abused, some were doted upon. Circumstances meant nothing. For all individuals who truly incorporated and grasped the concept of loving others, their past became irrelevant. Despite their own responsibilities and needs, they set others before themselves and gave, even if they seemingly had nothing to give. Were they revered in their lifetimes? No. A few achieved notoriety while they lived—mostly those who had the advantage of the media to broadcast their good works—but that isn't why they did it.

They did it because it was their calling to give love. Many people do it every day in other ways. There are legions of people who will get up several times a night to wipe urine and feces off the bottoms of other people, who would sacrifice their own lives for the life of another, who selflessly give and give and give unconditional love, for decades. You probably know such a person. She is your mother. Mother love is revered in our culture, even when it is imperfectly delivered by most moms, simply because it transcends the love most people have for one another.

So if this is all true, and as an adult you are not experiencing enough love in your life, what can you do about it? First, it depends on how serious you are. If you want to sit and whine and wait for someone else to bring you love, you will enjoy a long life of misery. If you want to connect to the divine, if you want to open your heart chakra to the potentiality of your ultimate mission, if you want to receive something more precious than money beyond your wildest dreams, then you must open your life to love.

The way to do that is to give love without wondering how or when you will be replenished. You can start today. You can start right now. As you give, as the energy of love, the energy of the divine, flows through your body and soul, you will find your soul expands to accommodate more. You will find it pours into you, that you cannot give more than love can. There will be more and more and more. As you help, love and serve others, you will minimize your own problems. You will create a better life for yourself, and your problems will shrink. Love is the power of the universe. It is the glue that holds humanity together, for without it we would slay all around us.

The love you have been shown is likely inadequate for your needs today. The way to shore up your deficit is by pouring out the old love you have been given, however imperfect, by giving it to others.

This is true and pure religion. It is the manifestation of your destiny. You don't need a channel to give you love. You don't need to write a book or start a movement or volunteer thirty hours at the local charity, although all those activities may become compelling for you later. What you need to do today is to put love on your to-do list.

You need to open your heart to love by letting the love in you come out. Recognize that it is a self-renewing resource, like air. The Bible talks about "gifts differing," which implies that each person is given a different ability. Those who can preach, preach. Those who can make the best brownies for the Girl

Scout meeting, bake. Those who can listen to a friend in pain, listen. There is no greater or lesser gift. All are crucial to the functioning and movement of love through the world.

Love giving starts out small and grows in accordance with what you've been given. Take stock of the love you show in a typical week. What do you do that's nice for others? Write down over the course of the next seven days what it is you do that's good and loving for another person. Did you pick up your friend's dry cleaning? Did you remember to bring flowers to your secretary for Secretary's Day? Did you volunteer to drive another person's child to school? Did you call your mother? Did you decide to do the right thing and refuse a dishonest opportunity? Did you say something nice about someone behind his or her back?

Write down the nice, loving things you do over the next seven days. Then think about how these make you feel. Do you feel more powerful, calmer, more patient, happier? Do you like the nice things you have done?

If you like them, could you do more next week? Could you become the most loving person you know? Could you become dear and wonderful and loving? How much effort does it take to wish someone "Good morning!" with a smile or to send a card to a sick person? The bigger manifestations of love will grow from your observations of the smaller ones.

I remember not being popular at all in grade school. All the usual complaints applied: My mom made me wear weird clothes, I wasn't good at sports, et cetera. The biggest surprise came when I realized with a start at sixteen, during my freshman year in college, that it was *me* who was the problem, not the clothes or the lack of athletic ability. I decided to study the popular kids at college since I was in a fresh environment for the first time. I would model precisely what they did, how they acted and how they related to other students. I'd see if that improved my popularity.

I noticed that the most popular girl on campus, Candace, was not only beautiful (something I could do nothing about), but she was also one of the nicest people I had ever met. She was gracious, kind and gentle. She was a good student, she always had good things to say about other people and she had a sweet demeanor.

The first six weeks of college were especially hard for me. I had to learn not to retort out of anger and pain when anyone said anything I didn't like. Guess what? Six weeks into college, Candace had taught me the ropes, and I doubt she even knew my name. I had friends and was popular for the first time. People wanted to like me, wanted to be around me.

It was at that time I realized something my mother had been trying to tell me my whole life. "You catch more flies with honey than with vinegar." What I finally deduced from this curious adage is that by being loving, kind, nice and friendly to people, I attracted loving, kind, nice and friendly people into my life. Like attracts like. Birds of a feather flock together.

This lesson doesn't stop when we leave school, but those who figured it out in school seem to get by okay in life, attracting and maintaining friendships all along the path. When later our lives yearn for a sense of spirituality, a sense of greater fulfillment, a sense of destiny, we sometimes forget to apply this crucial lesson.

Love attracts love. If you are feeling a lack of something, try giving it and see what happens. Try giving more love than you could possibly have inside you. In the minutiae of our existence, we forget the core principle upon which the universe operates:

love. Did you love another today? Did you give of your heart? Did you open yourself up to be there for another person? Were you a giver or a taker? Only in this space will we find the peace, love, joy we all seek in our lives. Only by making loving others a priority will we open our hearts and souls to manifesting our greatest destiny.

Becoming a BAV is a shift in your consciousness. It's a chance for you to personally create a warmer, friendlier, happier world all around you. It's the chance you've been waiting for to indulge your innate goodness and let it suffuse you and everything you touch with love, sincerity and goodness.

TEN

Socializing
Virgin Style

*If high heels were
so wonderful, men would
be wearing them.*

SUE GRAFTON, AUTHOR

Women become BAVs for as many
reasons and in as many ways as
there are people, but becoming a
BAV can be a lonely road if all your girlfriends are still out there screwing around. If
all the girls go out on Friday night on penis
patrol, you're going to feel pretty silly being
the only one in the bunch who is dancing to
the beat of a different drummer. You can feel

silly if you're not wearing the same kind of sexy clothes and getting the same kind of lascivious attention you used to get when you were available. You can tempt yourself into letting a loser into your life if you don't continue acting like a winner—and BAVs are always winners.

Women also can go into search mode (just like guys probably do) in other arenas. One of the current hot pickup joints is grocery stores. Women in search mode explore every nook and cranny of laundromats, bookstores, gas stations, dry cleaners, offices and other places with an invisible magnifying glass cloaked in the "secrecy" of nonchalance.

In reality, when you're looking hard, you're looking hard. Other singles pick it up or it wouldn't work. Like Victoria St. George said, as a BAV she picks up on-the-prowl energy in others quite easily. I believe when we are consciously not on the prowl we can relax and effortlessly allow in what is meant for us.

Many women interviewed for this chapter found sexual restraint provided them with an entirely new framework in which to view female companionship. No longer were they competing for male attention. Now they could concentrate on fun, conversation, and camaraderie with each other and with men. Their relationships with other women and their joy in being female were enhanced permanently by the decision.

Brenda reported, "We don't feel like all our energy is focused on getting a guy anymore. Now when we go out, it's just about being together." Tammy told me, "Not seeing other women as I thought men saw them—prettier than me, smarter than me, sexier than me—made me feel like I was part of a community of women who were all the same. For the first time in my life I fit in."

Deb said, "I find the only place not being sexual has really changed my relationships is with other women. My best friend divorced and quickly remarried. There was a part of me that didn't feel comfortable with the shift in her life happening so quickly." I think what Deb was saying is that she felt like her friend would have benefited from a cooling-off period, like the one she's created in her life.

Marcie told me, "My attitude has really changed my behavior with other women. Think about it: When guys want to go out with the guys, they say, 'I'm going out with the guys,' and they do it. But we give up so much time with our friends or doing the things we want to do. I'm pissed about that. Now I go out with the girls a lot. If he complains, I say, 'You do it to me!' I think women always try to put the man first and please him. We have to learn to have a life that includes more than him. After all, what are you going to do when they're gone?"

When I was a teen in Arizona, a wonderful old lady named Miss Fleming used to hang out with me when my parents had to leave town. Her tiny mobile home was heaven on earth as far as I was concerned. She had the rooms stuffed with pottery and beaded and knitted things she'd made. She spent her whole life indulging her many, many craft hobbies. Some of her work was exquisite and sold in galleries. I can remember sitting at her kitchen table learning how to make coral trees out of copper wire and red beads. She was completely content in her simple life, even though she was now in her seventies. She'd never been married, and in the blunt way of teenagers, I asked her why. "I never had a reason to," she replied. "I've always had a full life without any-one telling me what I could or couldn't do with my time." Miss Fleming was probably born around 1912. What a revolutionary she was, although I didn't know it at the time. She loved her life. She was always having people in for tea and homemade cookies, going to bridge games, and taking classes at junior college. My social life has never been as active as hers was in her seventies. Being a BAV isn't a sacrifice. It's a path to greater fulfillment and joy, a more profound personal experience than perhaps you have ever known in your life so far.

Almost all of us know a woman trapped in a bad marriage for decades who simply blossomed when her husband kicked the bucket. You think she's going to be devastated, but as it turns out, she's taking a chance she's never had. A very handsome Frenchman, Henri, living in the United States now, told me of his father's recent death. "We all thought my mother would have a hard time of it. He left her well-off financially, but you never know. He was such a strong guiding influence in her life. She never made a decision without him." The gentleman is barely cold and his widow is socializing with friends her husband never liked, involving herself more with her grown children, enrolling herself in classes. She's found a new lease on life. Her children are overjoyed.

> *Perhaps men should think twice before making widowhood our only path to power.*
>
> GLORIA STEINEM, FEMINIST, WRITER

Why wait until we become widows? Why not live vibrant, full, enjoyable lives while we are alive? Such sentiments were echoed in interview after interview: "If the right person for me comes along, fine. And if he (or she) doesn't, that's fine, too."

These interviewees were enjoying every moment. You, too, can learn to enjoy and savor the moment.

Now if all your girlfriends are still old-fashioned enough to be waiting for a man to start living, how in the world will you hang out with them and not slip right back into feeling like they do? One way to stay the course you've chosen for your own good reasons is to form a born-again virgins club in your area.

I like to write at Diedrich's Coffee Shop in Malibu. The place has "good energy." I often meet interesting people, allegedly by accident. While editing this book one day, a stranger sat down at the table next to me. In a few minutes, she asked me what I was doing. (Scribbling with a red pen and shaking my head a lot, apparently. After all, there is no great writing, only great rewriting.) I told her about the book. She exclaimed, "Oh, I believe in celibacy! Absolutely! It makes men treat you with dignity. Hey, are you interested in starting a group here where we can get together knee to knee with other women and encourage one another in this?"

There are women all around you who are eager to consider this option. I didn't make this up. It's a major national trend. You can find other BAVs all around you if you look.

We can help connect you to like-minded women if you contact our website *www.bornagainvirgins.com* or write to me at Health Communications, Inc. We offer online discussion group guidelines you can share. You can even form a real born-again virgins club in your hometown. We have a charter package with a newsletter, bumper stickers and a whole line of items to help born-again virgins claim their independence. You and your club members can literally become card-carrying born-again virgins. I'd love to connect you to women who are exploring the possibilities of life without sex for a while, and I'd love to hear about your experiences as you live your life with a whole new outlook. Write me.

Like Miss Fleming and widows who blossom into exploring their own interests, you probably have a number of activities you'd like to participate in "sometime."

You've heard it before, but here it is again: Take a class or go to a seminar on something you're interested in. You'll have fun, learn something and perhaps make new friends of both genders. Go without your "get a man" radar on. Now's your chance. All learning enhances brain function, which expands creativity. You can even apply your newfound creativity to your next relationship.

"Not being sexual with men has opened me up to being creative in my relationships," Bev said. "I apply energy that used to be spent sexually, as if sex was saying, 'I like you and want to get to know you better,' to saying it aloud. I wrote cards and even planned a little weekend getaway picnic with my new boyfriend Charles. For me, this is creativity enhanced by not being sexual—I am forced to be creative in the way I relate to this man. I find I am more verbally expressive, since we have decided not to be sexual yet."

Friends You Don't Need

Last month a rather handsome Italian-looking man was following me around the organic grocery store. When he intentionally bumped his cart into mine, I apologized and smiled. He took that opening.

He seemed personable, had several character traits that initially intrigued me (told me he was an artist: creative; told me he loves dogs: I have one; told me he is a vegetarian and believes in organic foods: similar lifestyle.) I gave him my number and left.

He called that evening and we chatted for about half an hour. In that time, I learned that he always has women screaming at him when he breaks up with them, that his ex-girlfriend wishes he were dead but he doesn't know why, that he believes the interior of all houses should be painted dark purple because it is "the most spiritual color," and that he is two months late on his rent but that he "has a nice manager." Bleep! Bleep! Bleep! Major warning signs! He also gave me a different age than the one he had shared with me at the grocery store.

I suppose I could have cut the conversation short, but I went from curious to mortified in thirty minutes. Yikes! He finally worked up the courage to ask me out. I knew it was coming. When he did, did I say what I think you should say in a similar situation? No. I said, "Well, I'm very busy this week. Maybe I'll call you next week and see if you're available." What I meant was "Don't call me. I'll call you." What he heard was "I'm interested in you. Can you please call me next week?"

So he did. Now I was ready. (I was coincidentally almost ready to write this chapter—okay, not so coincidentally!) I said, "Marco, I really appreciate your interest in me, but I just don't feel like we're a likely match, so I am going to have to wish you well, but I don't think we need to talk again."

Oh, gosh, did I feel mean! I would have been crushed if someone had said that to me. You know what he said? (You are expecting me to say he said, "Thank you for being so clear. God bless you and good luck in the rest of your life.") He said, "You stupid women are all alike! You play these (expletive) games with a man's head! I want you to know I have many women to choose from—you mean nothing to me. Stupid (mumbling)," and he slammed down the phone.

I shudder to think what would have happened if I hadn't figured out I didn't want to date this scary guy before the first date—or before I slept with him. I suspect very few men would have responded that way, but for your sake, and mine, I decided to ask a few single guys how a woman should say "Thanks, but no" clearly so that men get it.

Specifically, the question was "Let's say you meet some women you are attracted to. After a few conversations, or maybe an initial date or two, she has decided she does not want to see you again. What's the best way for her to let you know that so you have no ambiguity?"

Scott Friedman, a professional speaker living in Colorado, said, "Honesty is always the best policy, and we're all too busy to be spending unproductive time that will lead to nowhere. So what's the best way? Believe it or not, for me it's email. Just drop me a line, add a touch of humor if you like—or not is okay too—and tell it just like it is. Just don't be too harsh. It's not necessary to tear me apart. No real reasons needed, just something simple like 'I just don't see our kids spending alternate weekends with you after we're divorced. Thanks for the date, but I just can't picture us together.'"

Ed Scannell, a very successful author, businessman and trainer, said simply, "Honesty. A woman just needs to tell me honestly and clearly that it isn't working for her, and then we can become just friends. I'd rather know the truth."

Terry Brock, a technology expert from Orlando, said that when a woman is approached by a man and she's not open to it, she needs to say she is already in a relationship or too busy or not really available or something like that. "If she came straight out with her true impression and said, 'I think you're a little dweeb who is lower than maggot breath,' it might be considered offensive. I think best of all would be, 'I think you're really nice, but I would just rather not get involved right now.'"

Terry offered some additional helpful advice that all the men I spoke to echoed in one way or another. The worst thing a girl can do is smile and pretend everything is fine while he expends all the time, money and effort on something that he thinks is going to work. It would be much better to know up front and be friends, even casual friends, than to be strung out and pretend something is there that isn't.

Lawrence Kenna, brother of my lifelong best friend Lisa and a successful businessman in Winslow, Arizona, offered some insightful comments about *how* we can tell them. He suggested a frank declaration but that it be expressed in the form the relationship is beginning in. In other words, Lawrence suggests that if it's an email or telephone-based relationship so far, tell them through that medium. If it's already gotten to face-to-face dating, or even sexual, we need to tell them clearly, finally and face-to-face.

As every woman knows who has ever been "creeped out" by some guy who won't take no for an answer, some guys perceive no as a challenge. Lawrence offers this helpful advice if a man isn't getting the no part clearly. Lawrence warns, "Some men are simply trying to figure out what they did wrong or trying to win the woman back. Depending on the amplitude of the feelings, some communication may require a stronger signal and more profound rejection." Overall, he says, "Typically, a polite indifference is sufficient to end any further contact and can lead to a healthy limited mutual professional friendship or a valuable business contact in future years."

So what if you *do* want to date him—a lot—but you don't want to sleep with him (yet). How does a woman insist a man respect her decision to be celibate until there's a relationship supporting physical intimacy? Do you just come right out and say, "Look, I'm a born-again virgin—you heard about the book on all the talk shows. I don't have sex with anyone until there's a relationship."

Some guys will wig out, no doubt, and scream while running away from you. Great: that means fewer losers to sort out. Some guys will apparently think it's a challenge to their virility, the way some women find gay men a challenge to be overcome. They'll try all the more to get you to understand what you're missing. Listen to this story.

Big Willy

You can bet the names are changed for this story, but it's true, according to the woman who told it to me in incredulous giggles.

Penelope met Jon through a mutual business contact. She was not attracted to him sexually, but thinking she was being too critical, she agreed to lunch with him after he'd begged a couple of times. They were both in sales, so she admired his persistence if nothing else.

At lunch, he was charming: wonderful, witty, tender, sophisticated. Penelope was impressed by his panache but still didn't feel any chemistry, didn't find herself physically attracted to him. Being a BAV, she assumed this might be a good chance to get to know a guy without the distractions of mutual chemistry. She told him she was not being sexual with anyone until she felt like she was in a strong, healthy and serious relationship. Jon's eyes glittered, but he said nothing.

Jon invited her to dinner on Friday. One of their industry's biggest names was hosting an exclusive birthday party for himself, and Jon was welcome to bring a date. Penelope wanted to go for both business and personal reasons.

She arrived promptly on Jon's doorstep so they could drive the twenty miles to the party together. Jon wasn't dressed and answered the door in his bathrobe. There were candles lit all over the apartment, his version of romantic music playing, and chilling champagne and two glasses on the counter.

Instantly sensing she'd walked into a setup, Penelope felt uneasy. "I knew I didn't even want to walk into his house," she said. "He was suddenly creepy, but before he'd been so nice. It wasn't that I was afraid—he wasn't the rapist type. It was just that it was so obviously a ploy."

She walked in anyway, not quite sure what to do, and refused the champagne. He wasn't happy that she turned it down. "I asked him why he wasn't dressed, and he went downstairs to change, scowling."

At this point, Penelope prepared to tell me the grand finale to her dating horror story. "In a few minutes he calls to me to come downstairs and see his music room. I walk down the steps and it's one huge bedroom. He's lying on the bed naked, fondling his huge erection." She stopped at the doorway and just looked at him in horror. He said, "What's the matter, baby? Never seen such a big willy? Want to touch it?"

Penelope laughs now, but at the time, she couldn't get out of his house fast enough. Oh, yes: He never called the next day.

Thankfully, none of the other BAVs I spoke to reported such odd responses to their declarations of virginity. The reality of born-again virginity is—guess what—there are plenty of guys out there living this life, too. As much as it is easy to make them bad and us good, us virtuous and them mindlessly aggressive, I have to report that in preparation for this book I met more than three dozen men who are also celibate now, waiting for the right relationship before they will have sex with a woman, waiting until they know her well. Most of them mumbled something about "performance anxiety" if they didn't know they really had strong emotions for the girl, but they were talking to a woman when they said it. I can only imagine what would happen if they told their peers, the guys at the gym, what they were or were not doing.

These weren't geeky guys, mind you. They weren't men you'd classify as mousy or guys who couldn't fight their way out of a paper bag. They were real men, with real hearts, and real dreams of finding the right woman to share it. Does that surprise you? It did me. Doug Carroll, who wrote two articles on celibacy for the Valentine's Day 1999 *Arizona Republic,* was kind enough to let me interview him. He said celibacy is "a much more freeing way to live. It's an opportunity to get to know someone in a much deeper way. I think it ultimately dooms the relationship to put sex up front. When I'm seventy-five, who knows if the physical will still be there? But if all the other stuff is there up front in the beginning, I know it will be there in the end." I asked Doug how women responded to his declaration. He said, "You can sort of get a vibe from someone on how they feel about it from the way they respond. I couldn't even consider seeing someone who didn't feel the same way."

Doug wrote a wonderful article on celibacy, announcing his decision to the world, which took courage. It probably also took a different type of courage to face the bags of mail the *Republic* received in response to his article. Hundreds of people responded to his article, and their responses were supportive. Doug told me someone had this very metaphorical comment: "I'm tired of looking in the rearview mirror of my life and seeing all these bombed-out relationships. There's just got to be a better way." Maybe this is it.

In his article, Doug interviewed therapist Marilyn Murray of Scottsdale's Psychological Counseling Services. She told him that "a relationship's cord consists of four strands of intimacy—intellectual, emotional, spiritual and physical. If any one of the strands if damaged, so, too, is the relationship." Sex is stabilized in *intimacy.*

True intimacy, for men and for women, is the ability to be who you are—mentally, physically, spiritually and emotionally—and be taken and accepted for that in unconditional love by your partner. After all, isn't that what we all hope for anyway?

> *To share the flow of one's thoughts can be an even greater sexual intimacy than physical nakedness.*
>
> SOURCE UNKNOWN

Allison, the first BAV I met, described her decision to become celibate this way: "I was sick of the whole thing. If it wasn't going to be fulfilling, why do it? I was missing intimacy in my life. I didn't feel great afterward. It wasn't that sex wasn't fun. It was. But something was missing way deep down inside me. Celibacy taught me how to be intimate with other people—women, men, even my family and friends I've known my whole life. It taught me to be open and focus on other things."

Dr. Murray corroborated Allison's comments in Doug Carroll's article when she said, "Part of the mystique of seeing sex as special or intimate has been lost [in our culture]. People take sex for granted, rather than seeing it as something beautiful, designed to bring a couple together in the deepest way." One of her patients was quoted as saying, "We're so self-protective. We've had all this exposure to sex, but we've also been inundated with a type of psychology where we just protect ourselves. We're too afraid to say, 'Here's who I really, truly am. This is the pain I've been through. This is what I love. This is what I think about when I am alone.'"

In a relationship of true intimacy and trust, we can share our feelings. We cannot expect others to read our minds. We have to be able to say for ourselves, "I hate ice hockey" or "I love it when you rub my back" or "Please don't leave the door open when you come into my house" or "Ooh! That feels great!" Intimacy is being able to stay who you are and express your preferences. Maturity is then evaluated by your response to whether others do or do not agree to modify their behavior in accordance with your wishes. Will you compromise? Will you walk away? Will you negotiate? Will you fight?

It's one of the great advantages of the Internet that we get to be who we truly are before we meet people face to face. In former times, many men and women lived in small towns. They knew a lot about one another when they reached maturity and were ready to choose a mate.

During the Victorian era and later, men would come "courting" a woman. They got to know something about each other before the "relationship" really began. The Internet brings that back to modern people because it offers a chance for letter writing and candor. We are shielded from witnessing immediately the other person's response to our words. We don't see the looks on their faces. If your personal ad on America Online says you must have a man who likes to play croquet on Sundays and eat calamari, you are being clear, direct and honest about what you want. There's no need to pander to his needs and interests, as women might have done a generation or two ago, and because of the nature of electronic communication, it's easier to halt communication prior to meeting in person. Communicating your interests honestly is the only true ground on which intimacy can be built.

Doug Carroll further states, "You should consider celibacy if you've had trouble building true intimacy in relationships. I'm talking about getting to know someone from the inside out, soul to soul, and no shortcuts. Isn't that what we all long for— someone with whom we connect on the deepest possible level? Sex often gets in the way of that, if we're telling ourselves the truth. Sex can arrest the development of a relationship, giving us a false sense of closeness to someone. *Just because we're close physically doesn't mean we're in even the same area code emotionally or spiritually.*

"In a mate, I want intimacy in all respects and won't settle for less. Can't have that? Fine. I'll stay single and celibate." You go for it, Doug! Doug finishes his moving article with this extremely well-written statement: "Do some women think this is weird? I'm sure some of them do. And I'm equally sure some do not, agreeing that it's worth the wait. For the right woman, this would be the best wedding gift I could give her. If that sounds quaint, so be it. You see, *it's not that sex isn't important to me. On the contrary, it's important enough that I want to protect my heart and the heart of someone special.* Once this bridge is crossed in a relationship, there's no turning back without considerable pain. I've learned some difficult lessons there. I'm sure many of us have. *It's our own fault if we don't apply what we've learned."* Go, Doug!

How, though, do you actually draw the line? I mean, where and how do you express it? Take a look at President Bill Clinton's immortal definition of "sexual relationship" in which he didn't consider oral sex to constitute a sexual relationship. We know where he was drawing his line. A woman told me her very Catholic former boyfriend didn't consider it sex if only the head of his penis penetrated her, but the whole thing: Ooh—that's a sin. So he drew the line—and left her frustrated one too many times. She moved on.

Drawing the line is a fuzzy boundary for some people. Trying to be a good Christian kid, I drew the line at my shoulders. Kissing above the shoulders was okay, but kissing below was not, nor was touching, except for hand-holding. However, somehow this was a lot easier at fourteen than at thirty-four.

What boundaries are right for you as a BAV? How do you say "Oral sex only" or "I don't feel comfortable with more than kissing" or "I believe in waiting until I know someone better before I get physically involved in any way"? How do statements like that impact the person to whom you are saying them? How do you tell a guy you really like what you really want? How do you create and enforce your own limits?

Patricia Jakubowski and Arthur Lange are well-known in the area of assertiveness training. In their book *The Assertive Option,* they state that there are three kinds of assertiveness. The first they call *empathetic assertion.* That's where you acknowledge the other person's feelings without being mean or making them feel weird. It goes something like this:

> **DAVID:** Aw, c'mon, Lisa. You know how much I like you! What's stopping you? (He pulls her closer and kisses her passionately.)
>
> **LISA:** I know you're ready and willing to make love, David, and I like you, too. But I'm just not ready for that step yet.

If that doesn't work, other than the fact (if you're feeling gracious) that the guy is being a jerk or experiencing hormone overload, then we move to assertiveness type two, which Jakubowski and Lange call *escalating assertion.* This is how we deal with non-responsiveness from the other party:

> **DAVID:** Well, if you like me, and I like you, what's the problem? You know you want it, baby.
>
> **LISA:** I just don't want to move into it this fast, David. I want to be responsible, you know, and I want it to be right if it happens.
>
> **DAVID:** Right? What could be wrong? We're all adults here. I just don't see what the problem is.
>
> **LISA:** Problem? It's not a problem. I want you, too, but not yet.
>
> **DAVID:** What are you, frigid or something? You haven't been with the right man, baby.
>
> **LISA** (moving away from him): I said I'm not ready—not that I have a problem. I don't appreciate being insulted or treated like this at all.

One could guess that unless Lisa has very good reason, she doesn't date David again. If they do talk it out, he apologizes and agrees not to push her into sexual behavior until she's ready. On that condition, she agrees to dinner next weekend. After dinner, they are in the car when he makes yet another move. Now it's time for Lisa to move on to what Jakubowski and Lange call *confrontive assertion.*

> **DAVID** (while trying to unbutton her blouse): You look so hot tonight, Lisa. I love how this silk feels on your beautiful skin. Mmmm.
>
> **LISA** (pulling away and removing his hand): David, we've already talked about this. You agreed you wouldn't push me. Remember? This really makes me mad!

If you were Lisa's girlfriend, you'd call the guy a jerk and tell her to dump him. That may well be what she does. She also could make him take responsibility for his previous agreement and capitulate, if he's capable of it. His sudden attack of good manners might save what looks rather doomed at this instant.

Let's say it's getting pretty steamy. You've been touching one another all over, kissing seriously and are pretty far beyond aroused. Your body is screaming, "Take it to the next level!" but your mind is reminding you it's not so cool to screw somebody you're not completely sure about. Now what?

*We live in a society that trains
and encourages females to be victims of
sexual coercion and males to
victimize females.*

WILLIAM MASTERS AND VIRGINIA JOHNSON,
HUMAN SEXUALITY

Having been called a "prick tease" in high school, I cringe at
the thought of turning someone down after I've gotten him all
heated up. However, the reality is my commitment to myself and
to my virginity makes me feel like it's necessary even though it's
very, very hard to do. It's like being on a diet and getting served
a great big piece of chocolate cake. Can you eat just one bite?

At this point, your body language is saying, "Take me, baby!"
but your mind might be saying, "How did I get here and how
do I get out?" Take a breath, summon your willpower and say
aloud, "Wow! I really love kissing you, but I'm not prepared to
take this any further." Say it firmly, looking straight in his eyes,
with a bit of distance between you, so he knows you mean it.
You can also try, "Keeping my pants on is really important to
me. It's my boundary line sexually." Another option is to say,
"Now's probably the best time to tell you how far I'm prepared
to go with you. You can tell how attracted I am, but I feel comfortable going only as far as . . ."

The option is yours. Now, the other person has a right to be
disappointed, maybe hurt and maybe to plead their case a bit.
Remember the firmness and assertive statements we talked
about, though? It's critical that your actions and words at this

point maintain your standards. Otherwise, remind yourself what you will feel like inside tomorrow morning.

Allison and I had a long chat about her experience of telling men that she was celibate. "A number of guys really appreciated not having to go so far. I think celibacy didn't put me out there in the wrong way. When you can go home and keep flirting with someone, I think that's nice. The guys didn't have a reason to think I was a slut, and my girlfriends couldn't live vicariously through my life. It opened up lots of other things to talk about—with women and with men."

If you are going to date men while you are a BAV, and most of us are, then you need to know how to set and keep the limits you have set for yourself. Thankfully, Elizabeth Powell comes to the rescue in her book *Talking Back to Sexual Pressure*. She provides several examples of specific ways to deal with the subject. Incorporating her wise model might go something like this:

Linda and Kevin are in Linda's living room. They've been kissing and beginning to pet with clothes on. Linda doesn't intend to have intercourse at this time, even though she would like to. She thinks it would feel great, but she is popular and has dated a lot. She is looking for a long-term relationship. As attracted as she is to Kevin, she realizes she cannot go to bed with everyone she dates a few times.

LINDA (sits back on the couch for a moment): You feel so good! (Smiles.)

KEVIN: You, too.

LINDA: I need to stop for a minute. I'm very attracted to you. (She touches his hand, smiles.) I like this. This is great. But

I need to let you know how far I intend to go with it. (She stops to look at his reaction. He's listening. So far so good.) I hope you understand what I'm saying.

I'd like to keep dating you. I really like you. But I'll have to stop when it comes to taking our clothes off. Keeping my clothes on kind of helps me keep it under control. You know what I mean?

KEVIN: (frowning): Yeah, I think so.

LINDA: So that's what I'd like to have happen between us, to not go further than we have tonight. (She looks at him, concerned about his reaction, and smiles.) Would that be okay? Would you agree to have a relationship like that for a while?

Kevin agrees to give it a try or he doesn't and they separate. However, we're not always the ones saying "No! No!" and they are the ones saying "Pleeeeease!" It works both ways in the new millennium. Reverse her name and his, and the story remains the same. We hit on them and they hit on us. Ask any mother of a cute twelve-year-old boy. She'll tell you the girls call him to make offers. We don't have the market cornered on sexual issues, including celibacy or waiting for things to be right. The only difference is that women don't have a social model that *requires* they be sexually aggressive. Most of the guys I spoke with said there is not only a lot of pressure on them to be sexually aggressive, but that they feel pressure from the women they are with to make the first move, and it had better be an impressive one.

Cannot Handle Pressure

A few days ago, I met a man who seemed really charming. I was with others when we met, so I couldn't get to know him better, but I wanted to. Since I knew his full name and a professional organization he belonged to, I tracked him down. Finally, we spoke. I said, "You seem really interesting. Can I buy you coffee sometime?" He laughed. Nervous, I said, "It's not like I'm hitting on you, John!" He said, "That's exactly what it is. Now you know how guys feel!" He found it "highly flattering" that a woman would hit on him, and we agreed to meet for coffee. (Stay tuned for the sequel!)

If you've never asked a guy out, it's an interesting experience. The risk of rejection is high, no matter how much of a babe you may be or not be, because there are a hundred factors that could influence the other person to say no, from your appearance or personality to where they are in their relational development at the moment you make contact. Overall, though, it's still the guys who make the first moves, and I can assure you on their behalf it isn't always fun. There's plenty of pressure.

While driving home last night, I saw a billboard with large type that read, "Viagra is for wimps," and advertised a gentlemen's club below that. A "gentlemen's" club? I've known two women who have worked at these clubs, and neither would describe the typical patron as a gentleman. As for wimps, my goodness! Who could ever imagine that a man who has to pay to see naked women is anything but a wimp? Surely real men can get into real relationships.

While I must admit that for its audience the billboard was particularly good advertising copy, the message it sends to the tens of thousands of people who drive past it in a week is that real men pay for sexual excitement. Real men don't need drugs to get it up.

Although this book is not about the pressures on men to be sexual, the newest antismoking billboard in my neighborhood shows a Marlboro-style cowboy with a limp cigarette in his mouth. The caption reads, "Warning: Cigarettes may cause impotence."

However, it isn't our bodies that are working wrong; it's our hearts. When you're focused on the person you're with, the parts work 90 percent of the time. Men are under so much pressure to perform, though, and women are under so much pressure to be available that we end up with sexual dysfunction from trying to prove how functional we are. Does that sound as screwy to you as it does to me?

In their own ways, guys are under as much pressure as we are. For our part, we're supposed to be available and to be truly modern women. We should be able to do it without emotion. I'm sure some of us can, especially when we're "working off" life traumas and are in denial of our pain. The same is doubtless true for men. Still, most guys want what most girls want—real love and real sex in a real relationship. Why don't billboards advertise that reality?

I met a guy who criticized the concept of celibacy. He said what we need is for sex to be as casual and meaningless as walking past someone on the street. He believes it is women who confuse sex with an opportunity for intimacy.

I think he is in the minority. Take a look at the personal ads to see what I mean. Scores of men are writing how they are romantic, sensitive, kind, affectionate and fond of cuddling. Sure, some of them call themselves "hunks" or "studs" (the latter being an agricultural term for a horse or bull used for breeding), but most of the men talk about becoming "friends first" and "looking for Ms. Right" and wanting to get married.

Let's think about this. Millions of men out there are desperately seeking a loving relationship. There are millions of us seeking that. Are they all jerks, or has our society so screwed up our values that we can no longer recognize the true values of character, kindness, goodness, gentleness, charitable instincts, and the like in another human being? Are we judging all these guys against Pierce Brosnan or Brad Pitt or Leo DiCaprio or whoever the current hunk-of-the-month is? Are they judging us against Cindy Crawford, Farrah Fawcett, Sophia Loren, Gwyneth Paltrow or Amy Irving? Have we lost the ability to see one another? Could this be a factor of the cheapening of sexual relations in this country?

I met a real yenta this week, a practicing bona fide matchmaker. Sylvia Green of Malibu Matches asked me about my last relationship. I told her I had really cared deeply about Richard but that he was definitely *not* handsome on the outside. I told her he had a remarkable brain and a magnificent soul. She asked me how I transcended his appearance. I told her about this book. I told her my theory that when we're in our sixties it won't matter how sexy and attractive we were in our thirties. It will matter how much love, great conversation, companionship, acceptance and intimacy we shared. She smiled softly. "There'd be a lot more happy people in the world if we all had that attitude. One of the first things men and women usually ask me for is 'beautiful' or 'handsome.' It seems to me most men definitely want the looks. That's way up on their list. The women seem to want to hear beautiful things."

While we consider the matchmaker's observation for a while, let's consider what life is like for a man. Since I am not one, I asked some what their sexual lives were like. "I'm dating a new girl," twenty-nine-year-old Brett told me excitedly. "She's really great! She's nice and smart, and she is really good with her nieces. I think maybe there's something here." Brett tells me they've been sexual since their third date. The new girl, Shelly, is twenty-five. Please note the first words out of Brett's mouth weren't her bust size or how hot she is in bed.

Three weeks later, we talked again. Brett sounded devastated. "We broke up," he said, dejectedly. "She wanted to move back to Ohio where her family is." Brett, never married, didn't once mention how sexy this woman was or what a "stud" he was to catch a "babe" like her. I talked to Brett's friend Trevor. "Brett's really bummed," Trevor told me. "But I'm kind of glad she left. All he ever talked about was how she did this or that to him in bed, and how she likes his pecs."

Trevor was told one story, while I, the female friend, was told a completely different one. Which one is true? That's almost irrelevant. Both are likely to be true, but Brett has been conditioned to boast to his male friends about his conquests. If you catch Brett in a quiet moment, he'll tell you, "That's just how guys talk. It's got nothing to do with what I really want—which is a wife."

With that much pressure, someone surely has to step in and call the shots. Someone has to screen the good from the bad. It seems like a woman saying "Not until we're in a relationship" is sure of two things: getting attention from the right guys—ones who really want to be serious about a woman—and not getting attention from male breeding animals: the studs.

If we expect to be honored for saying "Not yet," this requires that we make a safe space for them to say "No, not yet" also. I believe we have little desire or motivation to be sexual repressors, and becoming a born-again virgin in no way is meant to construe that withholding sex means using our sexual power for evil or manipulative means. It is meant to honor who we are, who they are and what we are all capable of becoming.

You know how you feel the first time you are naked with a man? No matter how much you work out, no matter how much cosmetic surgery you've had, there's always one teensy little feature you wish were different. Guys feel the same way. They have their own insecurities. Imagine the relief they must feel when we take the relationship off the "Let's get physical" level and agree to see if there can be an emotional relationship prior to anything sexual.

John, forty-two, a creative director, explained his hesitancy to get physical right away this way: "I've had sex—I've had plenty of sex. I know what it feels like, and I know what I like. I'm in touch with my body and my sensual nature. All that's great, and it's important. But I see it as a spectrum. Over here on the left," he said, waving his left hand, "we have physical gratification. That brings pleasure, good feelings and nice sensations. That's great. On the right," he said, "we have meaning. We have that soul connection that can only happen when two people have the emotional connection necessary to really add something to the physical one. *That* is what I want."

John added, "Sex is cheap, easy to come by, totally available all the time. It's a common commodity—even animals have sex. But the emotional connection of two people *making love*, which can only happen when they've taken the time to really know, trust and care about one another, that's the rare, precious thing I want."

As a result, John lives his sex life by his own rules, admirable in a society that promotes promiscuity at every turn. He takes his time getting to know a woman. He begins the relationship, tests it, evaluates it, measures it, and only then makes a decision about whether or not he wants to have sex with the woman he's seeing.

His time frame? "Sometimes it takes months. Sometimes a bit less. I suppose if she kept pushing for sex, I would end it quickly. If a true emotional connection doesn't develop, I feel like I still have the option to make this woman into a friend, without all the psychological garbage former lovers say about 'Let's be friends.' By that time, we already really like one another, even if this isn't going to work in the long term romantically."

In speaking with dozens of men in preparation of this book, I heard many of them express the same sentiment, although not so eloquently, over and over again, and I have heard women tell stories of men who told them not to keep pushing. Do we laugh at these men who are so in touch with their feelings, or do we honor them? Society tends to laugh, especially other men. There are all sorts of hang-ups and surprises and feelings that could be handled if the intimacy to discuss them had been created before sex was scheduled.

"Jack and I were about to make love," Audrey said. "We felt like the time had finally come. We'd been dating for about two months, and we'd taken this weekend trip together. We'd slept in the same bed in the past but not been sexual. Not that we didn't want to be! On Sunday morning, he rolled over and woke me up by touching me. Pleasantly surprised, I allowed myself to enjoy the sensation of a man's attention, of Jack's attention. I became aroused.

"Jack pulled off his boxers and slid back under the covers. I wriggled out of my nightshirt. We kissed and touched and did that whole foreplay thing. It was really scrumptious."

They played around for a while, and "Then Jack went into the bathroom to get the condoms we'd talked about a week ago. I lay there in anticipation. When he came back, he didn't have them. And he wasn't aroused."

Audrey said she was so surprised at his sudden change in mood she just stared at him for a moment. "I'm sorry, honey," he told her. "I guess I'm not really over Rebecca all the way yet." Rebecca was the fiancé he'd left six months ago. He held her in bed, and they laid together in silence. Audrey was hurt, and frustrated, until she thought it through.

"Here was a man who wasn't going to schtupp me just because I was available," she told me. "Not only did that say that I meant something to him, but it also said he is capable of really loving someone and being faithful to that relationship."

Audrey decided to take a break from seeing Jack for a while, to allow him time to heal. They keep in touch by phone and email, and she predicts that a few months from now, they'll be back together.

Audrey easily could have been pissed off that she went home unsatisfied. She could have blamed Jack (in her mind or out loud) for not being a "real" man. Instead, she chose to see it in a loving, positive light. She's glad they figured out early on— before they slept together—how not over Rebecca Jack was. She's also glad that she didn't have sex and then have "those funny feelings" about being sexual, then wonder if the other person is being faithful, then wonder if she should be, and wonder obsessively if he'll get back together with his ex, and so on.

It is my personal assumption that as we move back to center sexually as a culture, as evidenced by the tens of thousands, perhaps millions of women who are BAVs, we will soon begin to "separate" people according to whether or not they are sexually evolved enough to say no to sex with strangers or to sex when it isn't within a relationship that suits their needs.

Different levels of varying kinds separate people on this planet. In this new millennium, we need to be very clear about the psychospiritual caste system we have collectively created. It appears that the people who are ready to honor their bodies and their hearts by choosing appropriate sexual encounters for themselves are the ones who are moving most quickly to the highest planes of existence.

ELEVEN

Staying Single and Loving It

*I've been married,
I've had kids. I did that part of
my life. I don't believe there's
anything left to learn there that
I can't learn out here.*

GARY S., BUSINESSMAN

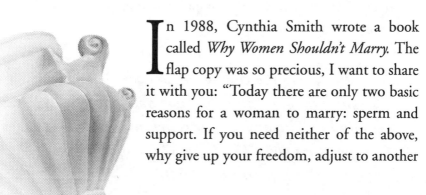

In 1988, Cynthia Smith wrote a book called *Why Women Shouldn't Marry*. The flap copy was so precious, I want to share it with you: "Today there are only two basic reasons for a woman to marry: sperm and support. If you need neither of the above, why give up your freedom, adjust to another person's lifestyle, silence yourself to accommodate a man's needs, become his domestic slave and emotional caretaker? . . . The 1980s generation of women are self-reliant, independent people who find living on their own fun and fulfilling. If a man is willing to fit into another lifestyle then perhaps marriage will be in their future."

Isn't that great? Whoever said we have to marry—or remarry? The answer is no one. If you don't want kids, fine. It's tough to raise them outside a marriage, but even having them inside one doesn't guarantee that help will always be there.

Remarriage is the triumph of hope over experience.

SOURCE UNKNOWN

If your biological clock isn't ticking because you've already done or don't need to have children, you may wonder what real benefits a marriage can provide. A great relationship can provide many of the same benefits, surely, as a marriage. Is locking your assets and time into a marriage the right thing for you? Perhaps a variety of friends, traveling companions and pals would be more your style?

Why buy the cow when you can get the milk for free, and the cow's only going to wind up sitting on your couch watching sports on your TV anyway? Or maybe I should say "bull."

LEIGH, JOURNALIST

So let's see. This gets back to need. Do you really need a man in your life right now? When my husband and I split up, I surprised myself by panicking about the things I had never done at twenty-nine. Call it silly, but the absolutely hardest thing for me to do was get in the habit of taking out the trash. I cannot tell you how many weeks of running down the street with a heavy plastic bag it took before I learned that every Wednesday night, I had a chore to do.

Let's take balancing the checkbook. It took about forty-five minutes to select the software, an hour to learn it and, ever since, I've been balancing five accounts all on my own.

As for taking care of the car, I am embarrassed to say that the idea of an oil change did not occur to me for almost a year, but the car, and I, survived.

Each single woman has an opportunity to weigh out the value versus the price of being married or in a committed relationship. So what exactly do we need a man for in our lives? A mentor of mine, Dr. Jeff Green of Pasadena, California, once told me, "There are only three reasons to be in a relationship: great companionship, great conversation and great sex."

The reliability of certain relationships makes them comfortable, but is your freedom worth reliability? That's a personal and individual question for each of us, but let's open it up for discussion now that we're BAVs and have the luxury of stepping back and observing our lives from a distance.

Why Women Shouldn't Marry

In *Why Women Shouldn't Marry*, Cynthia Smith writes, "So we have a marvelous generation of mature, achieving women coupled with a peer group of men who are Peter Pans. The reason so many thirty- to forty-four-year-old women have not married is they realized along the way, as they met and had relationships with these men, that the promised benefits of matrimony were illusory because the mature, responsible and loving life partners they were seeking were nonexistent. Maybe they always were, but previous generations of women were ill-equipped to quibble, so they compromised, they played dumb, they accepted the trade-offs. Because they had no choice." Thankfully, today we have a choice.

The reality of caring for ourselves motivates women "of a certain age" to work harder to provide for their own futures. Certainly the encouragement *by women* to use prenuptial agreements shows a base in reality that was not seen in our mothers, who planned to live their lives provided for by dad's steady job at the factory.

I can't mate in captivity.

GLORIA STEINEM, FEMINIST, WRITER

I've got to tell you a naughty little secret revealed only in the ninth chapter of Smith's clever book. The title of the chapter is "Closet Singles." Closet singles, by her definition, are women who never marry. She outlines three criteria: These women are attractive, they date widely and frequently, and they say they want to be in a relationship/marriage but never seem to "find the right man."

Aha! These women do not *want* to marry or remarry. Smith says of one woman she interviewed, "There will never be a Mr. Right because she doesn't want to be Mrs. Right but doesn't have the courage to admit that to herself, her friends or her mother."

Women like this often have men hanging around who would jump at the chance to marry them, but they scorn them, use them, and pick them back up to play. This very availability bores these women. The woman she interviewed listed all the things men she dated had done wrong or not done right. Smith points out that all those annoying traits are details wives tolerate because they consider the trade-off worth it. The woman she interviewed did not.

Smith cautions that this attitude of never finding Mr. Right, a Mr. Right who cannot possibly exist in human form, robs the closet single of being happy and accepting the joys of single life. She has to torture herself with an "eternal quest." Her constant searching and frequent failure create a sense of personal unworthiness and failure, which makes all her relationships—with males and females—unpleasant. She feels conditioned to believe she needs a man.

Wearing an apron and fuzzy house slippers with my second baby on my hip in my 1950s-style house, halfway through my twenties and halfway through my marriage, I was looking out from my picture window at women living the lives I longed for. I knew women who were living lives far different from the time warp I was in. It was a life I knew I could fulfill if only I were brave enough to take the chance.

The closet single is a component of that equation, except she's on the other side of the picture window looking in. She's secretly glad she's out there, and yet she wistfully observes the life on the inside.

In her classic book *The Feminine Mystique,* feminist Betty Friedan examined in detail why women had sold out for the comforts of suburbia. Why did they give up when such progress (at last!) had been made in their quality of life, freedom and liberty during the world wars? Friedan's classic work, and quotes from it, were background noise in my life as an American kid in the early 1970s. I have never known the universal societal bondage she describes, except through history books and the lectures of women a decade or two older than I.

Friedan compares life as a housewife to that of a prisoner in a Nazi concentration camp, arguing that both were progressively dehumanized. Both states inflicted a loss of identity as humans and destruction of self-respect, and both reduced their victims to a concern for primal needs (food, clothing, and shelter for themselves and their offspring). She states that she noticed women would say, "I feel as if I don't exist." This general suburban disease seemed to affect many of the women the young Friedan encountered. Both housewifery and prison forced abandonment of individuality and preference for the security of the crowd, both imprisoned their victims, cutting them off from the larger world of ideas and events.

Friedan's work helped to free women intellectually from bondage to men. It gave us the okay to have lives that didn't center around our husbands. Now we can choose to stay single, be single and hate it, be in a relationship or marry. Friedan gave millions of women a voice.

I suggest that the voice we hear now from the combination worker/mother/sexpot/domestic administrator/wife/stepmother/ PTA member we have become is saying, "I fear I don't have time to exist." We drive our sport utility vehicles filled with kids heading to ballet, karate and Little League. We race to work, we get up at dawn to make sure lunches are packed and the kids have all they'll need for their eight hours at day care.

Social revolution may well have overshot its mark. If sexual freedom is what we were seeking while thinking it is the universal panacea to all our woes, why are we not bounding joyfully down the streets, eager for each new dawn? If our station is improved, why aren't we generally happier, more fulfilled?

I remember a headline in a women's magazine of the late 1970s or early 1980s, "The Half a Loaf Life of the Working Wife." I can only guess what the article was about, but the headline caught my eye and has ever since been lodged in my memory.

When we add to that "half a loaf life" the pressures of divorce, the possibility of remarriage, all the concomitant needs when one reenters the single's scene (losing those fifteen extra pounds, buying new makeup and clothes, figuring out how to pay the bills and get the trash out on time), we find exhausted women everywhere. Suburbia has a new malaise. It is called chronic fatigue.

We've got it all, that's right: all the headaches, all the work, all the troubles of men, no gallant gentlemen to offer us their seats. The guy we met last month and slept with last weekend while the kids were at their dad's has no obligation to call again—much less any sense of social concern for our well-being. He can call, as we can, and drop us tomorrow for something newer, fresher, younger and more exciting.

How many men really get involved in domestic chores? How many of them do the cooking, stay home when the kid is sick, and make sure the family's diet is balanced? How many of them clean the house, pick up the dry cleaning or handle the myriad other tasks single women do every day?

The difference, as a divorced friend recently told me, between being married and being single is that when you're single you don't expect anyone to help you, so you cannot be disappointed.

I'm sure there are men who are exceptions to the rule. Still, in 1987 a study that interviewed men and was reported in *Why Women Shouldn't Marry* found that men feel their wives perform 80 to 90 percent of the domestic responsibilities of running a household. You have to wonder if it's changed much since then. What do you think?

At a fundraiser at movie producer Sherry Lansing's home last year, I heard Gloria Steinem speak on the rights of women. There were perhaps a dozen or so men in the audience. Steinem raised her voice and began to expound on the continued subjugation of women by men. Then, catching herself, she laughed, looked apologetically at the men in the audience, and said, "Of course, not you men here." Are they really still "the enemy" or is the old saying—"We have met the enemy, and it is us"—true?

Am I suggesting a return to the lifestyle of the 1950s? God forbid! I am thankful for the progress women have made. Indeed, it is a great joy to know my daughter and I function in a limitless world, although "limitless" may be overshooting the mark a wee bit. Like the pendulum that swings both ways, perhaps we won the battle and subjugated our captors. Now I advocate that we individually and collectively evaluate our singlehood or desire to remarry based on who we are as individuals and that we live our sexual lives consistent with our goals.

Have we fought, struggled and battled in such a way that we have gone from one ditch right across the road into the other? Are we mired in our own success? Do you really want to be married, or are you really happy single? Your choice is wholly yours, and it is easier to make from the vantage of the introspection inherent in being a BAV.

In her book *It Takes a Village,* Hillary Rodham Clinton discusses the fabric of U.S. society and its main building block, the family. Where is the family we need to create a healthy, cogent, abundant society in this time of astronomical divorce rates, rampant promiscuity, sexual confusion and STDs? You already know, as do I, that it barely exists.

As a part of this society, you have a responsibility to live your life in a harmonious way. If you choose to marry and provide a home for children, you have a responsibility to them, to yourself, and to society to give that home as good a chance of being a lasting and safe haven as you possibly can.

If you choose not to marry or you have children through marriage, adoption, single motherhood, a lesbian family and so on, you also have the responsibility to do your part to uphold the good of all. The United States is, after all, a huge melting pot, which implies we are all in this together. What affects one affects the whole, like a drop of food coloring in a bucket of water.

We moved from a society in which a woman's worth was her husband's bank account, or rather, we are in the process of doing so. We have certainly left behind a world where the ultimate career objective for a high school girl is to get married the June after she graduates. We are free to explore our sexuality, with little chance of real risk thanks to condoms and the pill, but have we built ourselves a newer, larger prison? Has our very liberty become our prison?

We now expect young women to have career objectives. We expect them to go to college. We predict they'll be sexual early. We have stripped them naked on the movie screen and on the beach, on billboards, in jeans commercials and in magazines. We have removed privacy, dignity and elegance. We have decimated chivalry and left ourselves with a quivering mass of manhood that is frightened to deal with us in our tigress masks.

With this sexploitation and media portrayal of the lascivious American constantly prowling for sex, one wonders if maybe the hype is getting a little old, if maybe the ease of availability has devalued the commodity. That is, if we can get sex anywhere, anytime, from almost anyone, what's the big deal?

As a culture, we have denounced sexual repression. Women make our own money, raise our own children, balance our own checkbooks, plan for our own retirements. We buy our own houses, we live our own lives, with our own friends and our own interests. While we are doing that, though, we wait for Prince Charming and fuck a lot of frogs.

> *If you want to catch a trout, don't*
> *fish in a herring barrel.*
>
> ANN LANDERS, COLUMNIST

What does it all mean? What's right for you, right now? Marriage is much easier to get into than out of, economically and emotionally. Making a mistake can really cost you big. Passing up the opportunity to marry might look like a mistake ten years from now.

Veronica, an acquaintance of mine, sat in the café with me. She asked to see a picture of my child. I showed her. She started to cry. I wasn't sure why. "I always wanted kids," she told me. "But always it was 'next year, next year, maybe next year.' Next year never came, and then it was too late." Now she's fifty-one and crying over somebody else's kid in a restaurant. She's got the money, the looks, the prestigious career successes. She made the best choices she could on her way up. What's right for you? What's wrong for you?

Nikki, forty-two, has been living with the same man who won't marry her for seven years, despite her pleading. Now she wants a baby before it's too late. His attitude is "Well, if that's what you really want, we should talk about it." Somehow they never do. In seven years, she's trapped herself in this relationship where she feels too stuck to leave and too sad to stay. If he leaves next year, she'll have no baby and no man. I wonder if she's thought through her choices carefully, before it really is too late. Would having a baby regardless of being married be the right choice for you?

How specifically would marriage improve your life? Think about this long and hard while you're living as a BAV. Marriage isn't for everyone, and on the other hand, maybe it is right for you. To present both sides of the argument, I quote again from Leanna Wolfe's book, *Women Who May Never Marry*: "Self-help books propose women need to take care of their own finances, career and self-esteem before getting involved with men. Women's dependencies are seen as overwhelming to male-female relationships. . . . This strategy disregards our human need for intimacy, whether or not we've worked it all out. It fails to address every woman's and every man's need to be held, to cry, to be responded to, to be cared for and to be loved. *Women and men who keep these needs on hold for a long time may be dying a slow death.*

"Contrary to these theories of self-reliance, relationships can be appropriate arenas for humans to work out their dependency needs. A relationship can allow us to address our otherwise buried needs to be dependent. All of us have unmet emotional needs from childhood. *Successful adult relationships team up partners who have complementary and/or compatible sets of childhood neuroses.* Two fully emotionally independent people would have no need to be involved with each other or anyone else."

What do you really want in your heart? Only *you* have to live with yourself every moment of the day, every day of your life. Why not meditate now on what you *really* want?

TWELVE

Climbing
Back In

*The poor wish to be rich,
the rich wish to be happy, the
single wish to be married and the
married wish to be dead.*

ANN LANDERS, COLUMNIST

For the vast majority of readers, born-again virginity will be a bright-yellow yield sign on life's journey. Most of us will choose to reenter a sexual relationship in the future, albeit hopefully more aware and in control than before. What might that relationship look like?

My daughter likes to watch the animated film *Thumbelina,* the clever version by Don Bluth. In this retelling of a classic tale, Thumbelina is stolen by a band of traveling frog musicians. The matriarch of the troupe, Mamma Frog, paints Thumbelina a vision of stardom—travel, money, the thrill of a cheering audience. She hands her the future like a glittering bauble, but Thumbelina decides she wants to go home and marry the prince instead.

Mamma Frog asks her why. Does she like doing domestic chores such as washing and cleaning and raising babies? Does she like cooking and scrubbing and listening to her husband talk? Thumbelina sticks with her decision, maybe because she's sixteen years old, but if you've been through a relationship before reading this book, you must admit the frog has a point. We all make trade-offs when we choose to be in a relationship. It goes way beyond agreeing to go to the movies when what you want to do is stay home and read a good book by yourself. While you've been reading this book, and perhaps living your life as a BAV, you've had a chance to compare the benefits and drawbacks of being in a marriage, in a relationship, and on your own. You are certainly ready to be fully conscious about whether or not a relationship is right for you now or at all.

One of my brothers called today. He's a late-twenties success magnet, working for a huge car company. He's kind, gifted and generally pretty sensitive. (Do I sound like a doting big sister or what?) We're all pleased at his amazing success. He was incredibly excited when he called—he'd just received a great promotion. They're transferring him. "What about Marge's job?" I asked, wondering if my sister-in-law was as excited. "Oh, she's thrilled," he assured me. "She'll take a new job in the new location or transfer within her (retail) company. We would just love to find any work that makes her happy." I cannot judge Garrett and Marge's decision as right or wrong—because I don't know what is going on inside their heads—but it made me stop and wonder when was the last time a woman called to announce to me that she was moving her family, husband and all, because of her promotion. Marge is a terrific, dynamic woman, yet our culture still supports being the male's job that determines a transfer.

Then you have Valerie. Valerie, who should be renamed "Valium," shops only at the best stores, because that's where the "best" men shop. She spends her second or third ex-husband's money and tells her lovers right up front she's a girl who likes to be treated well. If he doesn't have the right car when he picks her up, or if he doesn't know the right restaurant in Beverly Hills, he's history. She's caught "in between marriages." To my knowledge, she's been there for almost eight years. Time is running out to find another sugar daddy.

From birth to age eighteen, a girl needs good parents. From eighteen to thirty-five, she needs good looks. From thirty-five to fifty-five she needs a good personality. From fifty-five on, she needs good cash.

SOPHIE TUCKER, AMERICAN SINGER

How many single women have been attendants at one too many weddings until they finally say "Okay, I'll find a husband" and grab the first guy they can because the pressure to conform is getting to them? How many women conform to church, social, or family pressure to settle down and get married or crumble at last when their parents ask "When am I going to get grandchildren?" In our homophobic culture, some women even feel pressure to marry just to prove they are not lesbians.

While marriage is in part about choosing to compromise for the sake of love, I say that we should maximize our freedom while we are single. How many women have gotten tired of being single or lonely and said, consciously or not, "Okay, I'll take the next reasonable offer"? The expression "You get what you settle for" comes to mind. If we consider its meaning, we will see that it manifests in every area of our lives, perhaps especially in relationships.

What does love mean to you? Is it a kind, supporting, endearing commitment to share yourself and to accept another as they are? Will you know it when you see it? Will you jump at the first offer that resembles it?

Some women, and some men, too, live the term "a marriage of convenience" in its modern sense. I see these women on occasion. They are relentlessly buxom, tanned, thin beauties. Most of these formerly twenty-somethings married forty-something moguls. Their husbands are on their second wives and earned the economic ability to discard wife one for the newer, jazzier model. A few years and a few kids into the new marriage, wife two is not quite as fresh, young, or full of promise. The guys are sleeping with their secretaries, and wife two now yanks two small kids around in the sport utility vehicle. She gets her nails done and has her massage and somebody cleans her house for her. Her life of no action except lunch dates must surely be wearying on the mind. Her knowledge that he's probably gone on to the next catch has got to hurt deep inside, but his awareness that she probably married him for his money has got to hurt, too. She's got it too good to walk out, and he's run the numbers and realized that a second divorce isn't cost-effective. So they both look the other way and smile and continue their façade. This is a broad generalization, of course, like all observations. Sadly, it seems truer than people want to admit.

What life do these women have? Are they happy? Could they be happier if they "got a life" whether or not there is a man in it? I am sure they would be happier as BAVs.

Take a woman I admire greatly as a good example of how life can be. Deirdre Roney oversees the entire community service program at my daughter's school. This perky woman has at least two kids and one is a preschooler. From the size of the diamond on her hand, one could assume she could afford to float from lunch date to massage to aromatherapy. Instead, although she is not formally employed anywhere, she is using the comforts of her position as a wealthy man's wife to live a life of meaning and service. She is involved in half a dozen charitable organizations. She is an example of someone who didn't "marry for the money" yet got it, and she is making good use of the privilege it provides. She's a real inspiration.

In *Ten Stupid Things Women Do to Mess Up Their Lives,* Laura Schlessinger is right when she says one mistake women make is marrying the wrong guy. When will we get it through our heads that we don't *need* them but it's cool to *want* them? Half the problems of the world lie between those two words.

I married beneath me. All women do.

LADY NANCY ASTOR, ENGLISH POLITICIAN

I am not suggesting that marriage is a wrong or incorrect decision or that all relationships are going to be flawed and limiting.
Even with your girlfriends, you are forced into a position to
compromise on the time you have to yourself, the places and
things you do. For the friendship to work, you have to recipro-
cate by listening to your friend's problems when you might prefer to be doing something else and by being there for a friend
who was there for you. Friendship requires give and take, and
when the other person is taking, it takes that most precious
resource, the only nonrenewable one we all have—our time.

Those who would achieve great things would do well to give
their attention to the question of whether or not they are best
served by entering into a full-time relationship. More than that,
the question must become "How do I create an ideal supportive
relationship if I choose to be in one?"

The first step is to know yourself. Only then can you figure
out what you want from someone else. In his classic book with
the simple title *We,* Robert Johnson speaks of two circles.
Imagine two letter Cs made of iron. One is male, one is female.
They trip along through their lives and suddenly meet. The Cs
say to one another, "Wow! If I overlay your C reversed on my C
(reversed), then we will form a whole!" They try to form a chain
with what really are two open links. It's bound to work for a
while. Each has strengths the opposite letter C doesn't, so when
you lay them on top of one another, yep, they form a complete
circle if viewed from above. When you link them together at the
solid part, they certainly appear to be part of a strong chain.
However, in the inevitable jostling of life, the position of the Cs
changes and the weakest or open parts of the letters cause the
two Cs to split or fall apart: no more chain, no more strength.

The Cs married their opposites and now have found that the weaknesses don't support the long term.

Johnson states that for a wholesome, lasting link to form, one needs two complete links, each like the letter O. He means two whole, healthy, mature people who have dealt as best they can with their weaknesses. When they form a chain, these two solid links will create a bond that lasts.

This being true, how does one become a "whole link"? One uses a period of growth like the one offered by being a BAV, to invest in personal growth and the development of wisdom. Observe yourself, analyze your past and observe others around you. Use this time to determine your true goals, and acknowledge that whatever you choose is what is right for you. Many religious, spiritual and healing traditions value celibacy as a way of making oneself whole and healthy. There is no correct decision other than that which is correct for you. No third party can force you into believing that any course of action is best for you if you don't believe it yourself.

Remember Viktor Frankl speaking of his survival in a Nazi death camp in *Man's Search for Meaning*. He explains that what saved him when so many others lost faith and died were his hope in a future and the awareness that no matter what else his captors controlled, they could not control his mind.

The starting point for ending your experience as a BAV is knowing deeply why you want to end it. What criteria make you feel right with yourself? Are you sure the benefits of a relationship outweigh the benefits of remaining a BAV until further notice? If you are, then you must ask yourself what love is.

THIRTEEN

What Is Love?

*If marriage founded on love
alone is moral, then it follows
that marriage is moral only
as long as love lasts.*

FRIEDRICH ENGELS, PHILOSOPHER, AUTHOR

Assuming we want to be sexual only with a person with whom we are in love, we are left to define what love is for each of us. I believe it varies. For some, it appears that love is a willingness to be monogamous for a while. These people are laconically referred to as "serial monogamists." They occur in both men and women.

For others, love is a lifelong dedication and commitment to ever-lasting eternal bliss, in other words, a projection that will surely end in divorce or break up when the bubble bursts in a few years.

"Love," according to Ashley Montagu, "for far too many men in our time, consists of sleeping with a seductive woman, one who is properly endowed with the right distribution of curves and conveniences, and one upon whom a permanent lien has been acquired through the institution of marriage." Yikes!

> *It is easier to live through*
> *someone else than to become*
> *complete yourself.*
>
> BETTY FRIEDAN, FEMINIST, AUTHOR

A multimillionaire playboy had his pick of women. "Chad knew how to wow the girls," Brian said, chuckling. "He often had five or six competing for his attention." When Brian and Chad would go out for drinks, Chad would tell Brian "hilarious" stories of the way the women plotted to capture him and how vicious the war between rivals became. Chad would enjoy the women while they lasted and then let them burn themselves out and fade away when he tired of them.

Brian reported Chad's been with Linda for almost two years now. I ask why he's stayed with her and apparently given up his game. Brian laughed. "She's got the right benefits package: She doesn't want to marry him, she's got plenty of her own money, she's his physical 'type.' But more importantly, Chad's cheap. She pays her own way and since she's some sort of executive for a hotel chain, they get to stay free at the best rooms in four-star hotels all over the world. He says he's in love."

Burning Up on Reentry

I made a big mistake. Apparently, it isn't an uncommon one, but boy, did I feel stupid. After having been a BAV long enough to be really appreciating the benefits and really starting to understand how the process works to improve self-esteem, creativity and productivity, I made the ultimate mistake.

I decided I was ready to look for a good relationship. (That part wasn't the mistake!) It was a sort of spiritual decision. No sooner did I decide it than poof! A wonderful man named Richard showed up in my life. He was amazing. I figured it was destiny. He seemed to offer all the things I wanted in a guy, matching most everything on my wish list. He found it amusing when I told him I was a BAV and that we wouldn't be having sex. Plenty of time passed, and one night we were out together and began kissing passionately. The relationship had grown, I reasoned (in my mind only), to the point where I felt real affection and trust for him. I believed I was falling in love. In an instant, I reasoned that since this was at last the right relationship for me, there could be no harm in ending my virginity.

No sooner did I do so than I knew it was wrong for me. As soon as I had sex, I felt the guilt set in, and the rejection and the anger at myself and the person who let me down. Indeed, he did let me down because no sooner had we had intercourse than I truly understood he was still very, very much in love with his ex-girlfriend and that there was no room in his heart to love me yet. My assumptions on his availability were wrong. Not only did sex end what had the promise of eventually being a wonderful, loving, lasting relationship, but it also hurt both our feelings. He felt like he was betraying her, and I felt like I was betraying myself.

It's hard to tell this story, much less write it for everyone to read, but I hope that it will serve as a cautionary tale. I have never in this book set myself up as more than a reporter on a movement I see happening across the United States, but in my own efforts to live my life as a BAV, I let the cravings of my heart lead me into unwise choices.

I should have asked his intentions before I let it go that far, before I created a future in my mind that existed only there. It reminds me of a saying: "A lady's mind flits from the first greeting to marriage in only an instant."

So what did I do the next day? I reenrolled as a BAV—a little wiser this time. It will take more than a handful of wishes to make me risk making that mistake again. I am reminded of learning to ride a bike. I remember I fell down a lot, but I kept trying. Finally, I got it, and the rewards are certainly worth the effort.

I wanted to put that very personal story here to serve as a warning for you. Becoming a BAV doesn't guarantee the minute you're "ready" the ideal person will appear. It doesn't change the statistics on how many wonderful, worthy men are or are not out there. It ideally *does* give you a more macro perspective on yourself and others' actions.

As I learned the hard way, and shared so you won't have to, all that glitters isn't gold. Take this warning and these last few chapters as advice about "how *not* to burn up on reentry."

What Did You Mean by That?

One right we rarely if ever lay claim to is critical to our futures and yet hard for some to ask for. People have the unalienable, absolute right to know the intentions of the other partner before they have sexual intercourse. Is this just for fun or just to see what it feels like, or is it an expression of love and strong feelings for the other person? Guess what? Guys aren't likely to offer you this information on the "sperm of the moment." You get to ask, point blank, before Act I, because they already know. If they won't tell you, you can insist or cool it down. You have the right to informed consent, but you have to ask for it.

In her interesting book *Talking Back to Sexual Pressure*, Elizabeth Powell, M.S., M.A., offers a clever bill of rights for people who are clear and balanced about their sexuality. I repeat her material here with gratitude:

Sexual Bill of Rights

- I never have to please another person sexually unless the idea truly appeals to me.

- If anyone rejects me for my sexual beliefs or preferences, I can survive and very likely find another person.

- I am an adult and I can take care of myself even if I have to be alone for a while.

- I am capable of speaking up when I see a sexual risk, or a chance to improve my sexual relationship.

Ms. Powell goes on to state, "If deep down you believe these things, you will feel calmer and more able to cope."

Potato-Vine Passion

Mary met Greg across the fence dividing their homes six months after she moved in. She'd never seen him before, except from a distance. She was wearing no makeup and a dirty gray sweatshirt and was sitting eight feet up in a tree pruning a branch when she first saw him up close. It had been about three years since she'd seen a man who interested her.

He came over to chat about plants that grow well in the area, presumably. From her perch, she could see he was remarkably cute, even in dirty jeans and a paint-stained work shirt. She knew he was single.

After a lengthy discussion about potato vines and star jasmine, he offered to email her some information on regional planting schedules. Doesn't sound like much of a romance to you? In the beginning weeks of their friendship, Mary said they both frankly discussed their desire to wait and their surprisingly similar reasons. Both were experienced enough to know what they were missing and what they were gaining. At last report, their as-yet-to-be-sexual relationship is going strong and they seem as happy as, well, two peas in a pod.

Knowing who the other person is before you become sexual and knowing that person's intentions are critical to achieving your relationship objectives, no matter what they are. The next thing for you to know is what kind of lover you are.

What Kind of Lover Are You?

Does this subject seem out of place in a book on celibacy? It shouldn't. If you choose to be celibate, the only reason you're likely to come out of it is for what you believe is real love. So what kind of lover are you? What kind of lover do you want? What kind of love best suits your personality? What you mean by love and what some guy means by it could be two totally different things.

Have you ever noticed there are some people who can say "I love you" to people they don't even know and others cannot say it even to people they love? Before I was a book agent, I worked for a while in Hollywood selling screenplays. I assumed the stereotypical agent affectation of using the word "love" in every sentence, as in "I love your work" and "Love ya, baby." Love, love, love. What does it really mean? It meant nothing to the people I was saying it to every day, and it meant nothing to say it. Some people are like that in the language of romantic love, too. Glibly, they hurt others' feelings.

The Greeks have at least four words for love. How clever of them. There's *koinonia,* which is friendly love. Some people want to marry their best friend. It's like group love, a warm fuzzy feeling sort of thing. Then, there's *agape,* which is transcendent, godlike love. This is the love a being has for a deity and the love the deity has for the human. It is the love the Bible says motivated God, as in the phrase "And God so loved the world that he gave his only begotten son."

The city of Philadelphia, where this book was conceived, is named after *philia,* which is the Greek word for "brotherly love." That's why Philadelphia is called "The City of Brotherly Love."

This brotherly love is the love you have for your family members. The fourth type is *eros,* which is sexual love. That's the chemistry thing. That's what most people think of first between a man and a woman—the kind of love that gets people into bed.

So what do you mean when you say "love"? What does your man mean when he says it to you? What kind of love do you want in your life? Each type of love translates into a different type of behavior. Which one makes you happiest? Remember what I told you about my mentor Dr. Green, who once told me, "There are only three reasons to be in a relationship: great companionship, great conversation and great sex." How these three show up for you, based on your needs and desires, determines the happiness factor in your relationships.

We all want some of each, but if you think about it, one aspect is probably predominant for you. There's nothing better or worse, only ways of deciding what honestly is right for you. What works for one woman would drive you nuts. Think about the following types and notice which attracts you most:

There's *friendship love.* People interested in this type of love want their lovers to be their best buddies, to be on the same wavelength as much as possible. Someone who prefers this type of love would probably want to be with a man with whom she can really talk and share activities and ideas. This couple would see the family they create as their primary social unit. They tell friends, "I married my best friend."

There's *self-sacrificing love.* That's the kind that women on television in the 1950s seemed to model. Sacrifice everything for the good of the family. Be a martyr to the relationship. As long as he's happy, she's happy, too. For women who choose this kind of love, a dictatorial, controlling guy is just fine. He gives his orders and she follows them. Some women equate this with a feeling of security, relief at not having to make decisions or a sense of being protected.

In *chivalric love,* women want to live in a fantasy of intense erotic attraction, romantic candlelight dinners and chivalry forever. Good manners in a man are very important to such a woman. Her ideal guy would probably need to know to walk on the curb side of the sidewalk when he's with her, pick up most of the checks, bring her flowers, that kind of showy stuff. She probably read lots of romance novels in high school. He'd better be a hunk, at least in her eyes, or she'll keep looking. Lots of single women are still waiting for this kind of fairy tale to have a happy ending.

Logical love is practical. You absolutely want your man in your life, and you know precisely why. You feel your assets and his complement one another. You have goals and you see this person as a partner in helping you achieve them. There's no fluff in your decision. It's based on reality and facts. You are very practical about the person you love, seeing strengths and weaknesses, comparing them to your own, and expressing your love in practical ways. You will appreciate the blender he gives you as an anniversary gift in five years. Chances are, you're the type who believes love is just a word but actions speak louder.

Codependent love is when you feel most comfortable being intensely needed by your partner and intensely needing him. When you want to spend every waking moment together, when you expect three calls a day from him at his office, you've got codependent love. You feel like you'd die if he left you, and you worry about him finding someone else. You're happiest together, so you're together every possible moment. You drop outside interests and friends to focus on the relationship.

Narcissistic love is when you are—or he is—the center of the universe. The most immature form of love, this is how babies express themselves: Everything they want should be theirs, right now. Adults who evidence this type of love generally were maladjusted as children and fail to recognize the need for reciprocity in mature relationships. These are the people who whine at you to do things for them. Some people like to feel needed by needy people, so they go for narcissistic love.

People choose different types of love based on how they are feeling about themselves at any given time. As a BAV, there will never be a better time to sort through past relationships and determine what type of love, if any, was most prevalent. Then you can make new decisions about whether or not what you've done in the past is working for you today.

I suggest you try this exercise: On a sheet of paper, write the names of the men to whom you have said, "I love you." Include your father and brothers and other significant men in your life. Then go back and determine which of the types of love of the six mentioned above you felt predominantly for each man. You will see you loved some men in more than one way. Choose the type that most clearly defines the *majority* of each relationship.

You will likely see an interesting pattern. Ask yourself if the types of love you have most often been involved in are appropriate for your optimum mental and emotional health. You have the opportunity while you are living as a BAV to reevaluate your past relationships, to make new decisions and to prepare to try again. I suggest you either seek professional counseling or read books on the type of love you most often create if you are not happy with it. You will truly never have a better time than now.

Testing Your Love

Here's a simple test to help you determine which of the love types we've just discussed best describes your personal style. Of course, you can change your style at any time you choose, but it is helpful to find out what sort of love style you adopted in the past. Then you can decide if it worked well for you or not.

All you need to do is answer the true or false questions as best you can. Think about your most recent meaningful relationship when you answer, or what your ideal relationship would be like. There's no right or wrong answer. Being a BAV is about knowing yourself and what works best for you. This test will get you started. Scoring follows the test.

1. I am friends with almost all my old lovers to this very day.

   ❏ True   ☒ False

2. The very first time we touched, I knew love was possible.

   ☒ True   ❏ False

3. Love only develops after you've cared about one another for a while.

   ☒ True   ❏ False

4. I like to keep my partner just a little insecure about how much I care.

   ❏ True   ☒ False

5. I consider carefully practical things like a potential partner's expected future earnings before I commit myself emotionally.

   ❏ True   ☒ False

6. I recognize that to be truly loving often means sacrificing my wishes and goals for the good of the relationship.

❏ True ☑ False

7. I'd let go of someone I loved if I thought they'd be happier elsewhere because my partner's happiness overall is a critical thing to me.

❏ True ☑ False

8. I have had more than one lover simultaneously, but they didn't know about each other, and I made sure it stayed that way.

❏ True ☑ False

9. If he brings flowers on the first date, I know I'm going to like this guy.

❏ True ☑ False

10. I like my lover to keep in touch several times each day.

☑ True ❏ False

11. I score my partner against my wish list and keep records on what has worked in past relationships.

☑ True ❏ False

12. The best kind of love grows out of a long-term friendship first.

❏ True ☑ False

Okay, are you ready? Following are the scoring guidelines. Remember, this is not a clinical test, but it's sure to give you an indication of your own preferences. You may surprise yourself.

If you answered "True" to 1 and 10, chances are *codependent love* feels most comfortable for you. You don't just want love. You need it to feel whole.

If you answered "True" to 2 and 9, chances are that you are a natural *romantic lover*. You probably think secretly that Cinderella endings are possible—and charming.

If you answered "True" to 3 and 12, chances are you value *friendship love* highest. You probably really like a lot of people and can't quite say how that one day becomes love for you.

If you answered "True" to 4 and 8, you should call Copernicus right now and tell him you've found what Earth really revolves around—you! You are a *narcissistic lover* and are perhaps not ready for something serious—yet.

If you answered "True" to 5 and 11, you're a *logical lover* in the way you use your emotions. While you may not be Dr. Spock from *Star Trek,* you're certainly going to look (with a magnifying glass) before you leap.

If you answered "True" to 6 and 7, you're a *self-sacrificing lover,* ready to be burned at the stake as a martyr for your love. You believe at some level that "love hurts."

If you scored the same in two or more areas, give some real thought to your relational style. Which feels instantly most comfortable? Which would you advise your best friend to pursue?

Whatever kind of love you feel is best for you now *is* what's best for you now. No one has the right to judge you, and it takes all kinds of people to make the world. Once you know what kind of a lover you are, you are much better prepared to determine what kind of lover you want.

Making a List and Checking It Twice

In an earlier section of this book, I presented the choices made by Queen Elizabeth I and how that related to focus. Elizabeth I refrained from sex because she wanted to focus on building her life exactly the way she wanted it. Isn't it true that if you focus on what you want, you have a much better chance of getting it, especially if you don't waste your time exploring the options that aren't what you want? Is that what you are doing?

Many relationship books talk about making a list of the characteristics you want in a potential mate. I think that's a great idea, and I have made a list for myself. I have thirty-eight qualities I'd love to see in a man. I don't expect to find someone with all thirty-eight. The hard part for me is focusing on that list. Sometimes, I will meet someone and, based on the first conversation or date, I will see things that aren't there. It's hard to focus on the real person and not my own wishful thinking. Sometimes I have ended up dating someone because I lost my ability to focus. In my own life and in researching this, it seems that at about twelve weeks in a nonsexual relationship you really have gotten to know someone. Perhaps this is why employers have a ninety-day trial for new hires.

How do you create a list of "features" necessary for you to be in a happy relationship? After determining the kind of love you want from the categories below and determining what types of relationships you've had in the past, you will be much clearer about what you want in the future.

Here's how to make your list:

Take another sheet of paper and—this is *so* important—write down the characteristics and physical traits you like best about yourself. You could say, "I'm philanthropic, I have nice hair, I am nice to animals, I am sensitive to other people," and so on, or get out your 3 x 5 cards. Remember Robert Johnson's analogy about the letter C links? You absolutely want a man who has your good traits, so those are the first things that go on your wish list.

Next, think about the things you really hated in people you've known. (By the way, psychologists say that we respond most dramatically—positively or negatively—to the traits in others that exist in ourselves. I used to despise people who talked too much until I realized, oops! I do that same thing! Just come to one of my seminars and you'll see for yourself.) Think about the negative traits you see in people you know. Examine yourself honestly. You're a BAV, sister! You've got time to invest in your own growth. Could any of the traits you despise in others exist at some lesser level in yourself? Do you fear being a certain way even if you're not?

After you've considered negative traits that bug you, write out what the opposite of each trait is. Let's take my example of "overly talkative." The opposite is quiet. Gee, I would hate to be with a guy who is quiet. I'd be bored in a second. What do I really want? I want someone who can listen as well as talk. I love talking, but I can only learn when I listen, and I love to listen. After reflection, a man who can listen went on my list. See how it works?

You are building a composite male based on your own personality, needs and desires. If you have zero money and have never set foot inside a Bloomingdale's, Bergdorf Goodman or

Neiman Marcus, it's a little unrealistic to hope to marry a multi-millionaire—although it's remotely possible. If you set your sights on a rich man, you'd want to invest energy in learning two things: how to make money and how to dress tastefully, which might mean investing more energy in yourself before you rush out of being a BAV. The idea is you become a BAV because you honor and like yourself and because you have the personal dignity to be self-sufficient. Why rush right out and jump into the arms of someone else to "fix" your life for you? Fix your life and character, or at least be making progress, before you go looking.

As you think of characteristics you like, write them on your list. Each woman's list will have different things on it. I am an analytical person, so I actually rate men on the list when I meet someone I might possibly be attracted to. I "score" them on the first encounter, the end of the first week of knowing them and then again at various times during the time I know them. I watch as I gather more information how I determine that this one isn't kind after all, that one is actually much more polite than I first thought, and so on. This method is teaching me not to trust my tendency for love at first sight. For someone like me, that's a good thing.

Once you know what you believe you are shopping for, it's easier to go to the grocery and get what you want. Most people believe God or the universe or karma or destiny brings people together at the right place and time. With a clear idea of what you are looking for, at least you have a better chance of recognizing it when it shows up. Use your list as a parameter, not a ruler.

Of course, as with every great debate, there's an opposite position to the concept of making a list of characteristics one's potential mate should have. I found it best expressed in *Women Who*

May Never Marry by Leanna Wolfe. She writes, "Many of the single people I interviewed had extensive wish lists for their prospective partners. . . . People . . . ask for so much because they are used to getting what they want . . . in our intensely consumerist culture . . . another reason . . . is inflated expectations," which she says are encouraged by *Playboy,* Barbie and Ken. Are your wishes realistic? If you can honestly say "If I don't get the items on this list, I'd rather be single!" then don't complain about being single.

If you've been single for years and years and the problem is there always seems to be something wrong with the guys you pick, with whom you are initially in love, sister, the problem is you. None of us are perfect: not you, not him. Remember when we discussed compromise?

Becoming a BAV offers you the opportunity to fall in love with yourself, to accept yourself. I have a friend we'll call Ginger. She is particularly attractive, but for years she did not perceive herself that way. She is one of those women who demands perfection in her appearance or else feels like a total failure. When menopause approached, she suddenly developed a less than flat stomach and a few pounds of cellulite. Panicking, she exercised like crazy, but short of liposuction, she is under the impression it's there to stay.

Recently, Ginger made a developmental leap, if you ask me. She had always dated the best-looking guys, who were generally little deeper than their perfect skin. They, like she had, lived for their appearance. Now, suddenly faced with her own mortality, what's a girl to do? Ginger went through about six months of introspection. She decided that since her old ways weren't working, she would change. She had always been intrigued by amazingly bright men but had never actually dated one, because typically they were not hunks. So she tried it—and guess what? Once she stopped focusing on her appearance or how she felt people were looking at her date, she developed wonderful friendships with several men who are not "hunks" and in two cases may even be less than average looking.

Ginger said, "I just realized that there was more to me. Once I recognized that there is more to who I am than how I look, I started looking for people with good souls, good minds, charitable hearts, and I stopped making the entry criteria for someone I could love so high."

Did Ginger lower her standards? Some might say yes. They might say she gave up the fight, but I see it as maturity. She went from an obsession about herself that she applied to everyone around her (narcissistic love) to accepting herself and thus everyone around her. What an interesting example she is setting.

Remember Allison—the woman who sparked this book idea? What a wonderful story she has to tell. "I'm on the road to being so healthy!" she told me exuberantly. "I dated this guy for four months before we did anything, and now we're in love! He never pushed me to have sex. He even said, 'If this works, we'll have our whole lives for that.' Today, I am totally in love. We built a strong base of emotional intimacy before we had sex. He's a gentleman, so romantic, he opens the door for me, and walks on the curb side of the street. *That's not important to everyone, but it is important to me* (emphasis mine). I know he adores me. I cannot believe it! I didn't even really want this in my life—I wasn't looking, I was content with celibacy. . . . The great thing about waiting is that I don't feel like I have anything to hide. I have the freedom to completely and honestly communicate with someone. I feel so fortunate I found this. I asked myself, 'Is it me or did he make me this way?' It's me. I changed the way I trust people."

She found her man and she's happy with the dignity she created for herself and the trust developed in the relationship before it became sexual. Although they don't live in the same city, they see one another several times a month and one day he will probably move to San Francisco to be closer to her. Allison said, "When I met Jeff, we just kissed and held hands for hours. Sometimes we talked, sometimes not. We even slept in the same bed and just kissed. He was experienced sexually, so he really loved the intimacy we created without the sex. Even now that we're lovers, we've sometimes spent two or three days together and not made love, because it isn't about penetration or the cum shot for us. I feel like we're making love even when we're not in the same room. It's wonderful!"

Allison, the first born-again virgin I ever met and the one I introduced you to first in chapter 1, is living her happily ever after.

FOURTEEN

Sex Education
for BAVs

Keep your knees together . . .
change your life.

WENDY KELLER, AUTHOR

Great sex in a great relationship is grand. It's an excellent goal for people who have consciously decided that's what they want. It's ideal if both partners enjoy compatibility with one another and find joy in their sexual experience and in one another. Both people have what they want, but apparently at the top of some guys' wish lists is finding a nymphomaniac.

In their 1964 book, *Nymphomania: A Study of the Oversexed Woman,* Drs. Albert Ellis and Edward Sagarin say, "Many men dream of finding a nymphomaniac, and look upon her as a boon, but they are actually thinking of an easy-to-seduce woman—*not* a nymphomaniac. The seduction of a male by a compulsively hyper-sexed woman (with whose emotional disturbances he is no way prepared to cope) can be a serious problem to *him*."

Being a "nympho" is U.S. slang for a woman who is always turned on and ready, but at what price if her heart isn't lying on the bed with her body? The price is her soul.

I remember male friends telling me with great joy that the woman they were seeing was a "nympho" or that such was the type of woman they would settle down with—one who wanted at least as much sex as they did. Apparently for some men frequency of desire is a macho thing.

Some women can reach orgasm while sleeping, even when the guy is nowhere near and perhaps has never even touched them. In the early days of a sexual relationship, or the first days or months of living with someone, the enthusiasm, the anticipation, the excitement and dreams can cause us to be more sexually excited both mentally and physically. Over time, however, as the excitement wears off, other things, like technique, might need to come into (fore)play.

From the perspective of maturity, I observe that in the beginning of a new sexual relationship between trusting, loving friends, frequent sex is a common desire for both partners. Little by little, unresolved issues, concerns about the relationship, the birth of children, the onset of extreme stress and the expansion of responsibilities tend to modify sexual excitement. In some cases, this shift may occur because familiarity breeds contempt.

In any case, normally (not ideally, mind you) every relationship will experience a natural decrease in frequency of sexual contact, especially between partners who live together. A woman who was a "nympho"—labeled such either by her husband/boyfriend or herself—may find herself no longer in that category.

In an ideal world, no heavy responsibilities, no daily cares, no constant worries, no nagging doubts, insecurities or struggles in the relationship would mar perfect sexual harmony. However, let's be honest. If you're mad at him about something, or even just disappointed, isn't it harder to feel sexual toward him? Maybe impossible? Then the fact that you are no longer a "nympho" is a barometer of the intensity of the relationship, not a reflection of encroaching frigidity or something wrong with you.

I could go so far as to postulate that if you are feeling less attracted to your man and he still wants to jump you (for that is what it has become), his persistence without addressing the underlying causes for the reduction in your libido is at the very least as much *his problem* as it is yours. It reminds me of a "guy joke" I heard, and the reality of it is too sad not to be brought out here:

Two men are sitting in a bar, drinking too much. One is complaining about his wife. "When I get home from a night of drinking, I park the car two houses down so not to disturb her sleep. I tiptoe up the steps and barely scratch the key in the lock. I undress in the bathroom, creep across the bedroom carpet and noiselessly slip into the bed. But every darn time, she wakes up and starts yelling at me. 'Where've you been all night?'" The guy collapses his head into his hands miserably.

"Cheer up, pal," his buddy says. "You've been doing it all wrong! When I get home really late, I screech into the driveway, slam the front door open, grab a beer from the fridge, stomp up the stairs, turn on the bedroom lights, pile my clothes in the middle of the room and jump into bed stark naked. Then I yell, 'I'm home! Let's screw!' And you know what? She's always sound asleep!"

This joke is an exaggerated example of women's sexual behavior. Most men are not boorish slobs. They are, perhaps, even largely well-meaning. One can only say for certain that the ones who are conscious (and if you are conscious enough to read this book, you are not the type of woman who would ever tolerate one of the men in the joke above) would also prefer a wholesome, happy, harmonious relationship with you. They want it to work, ladies, just like we do. Just somebody, probably us, has to step up to the mike and tell it like it is.

We are the ones who have to take responsibility for our relationships—both their formation and their nurturance, not because men are incapable or unwilling (even though they have been acculturated to believe they are both) but because we must take responsibility for the things we do not like in our lives and create the impetus for change, just as we must in any aspect of life, regardless of gender.

Some women actually experience encroaching frigidity in their marriages, even after previously satisfying relations. This leads them to assume that the marriage is over, the love is gone, or there is a problem with themselves or their mate. This causes a lot of extramarital cheating—the woman doesn't respond like she "used to" or "should," from the male's perspective, because the relationship has been marred emotionally or physically. In other instances, she cheats because she just "doesn't feel attracted to him" anymore.

The outgrowth of frigidity can become blatant sexual behavior after divorce—or the so-called "crazy time" in which many newly divorced people rush around trying to staunch their emotional pain and prove their physical aliveness and attractiveness by basically screwing anything they can get their hands on. Without wisdom, these new "relationships," too, will come to ruin eventually.

> *The worst part about running*
> *from your problems is that you have to*
> *take you with you when you go!*
>
> SOURCE UNKNOWN

Sexuality is largely mental, as we know. Research with paraplegics—those paralyzed from the waist down—conclusively shows that they experience orgasm much as they felt it when they had functioning in their lower bodies. What can explain this? Only the truth that the brain is the largest sex organ. Sexual pleasure is mental. If you've ever been sexual in your life, you know that there are times with the same partner when you are into it and times when you are not. It would appear that the satisfaction from the sexual act itself is largely mental in nature. Lack of psychological compatibility is probably the main cause of sexual incompatibility.

In my research, I also found a physical reason for the phenomena of relentless promiscuity and the inability to reach fulfillment. This interesting discovery is that if one knows her body well enough to be able to find sexual fulfillment *whenever* one is sexual, or learns to do the same, two psychological benefits occur: (1) It is no longer mandatory to "test" sexual compatibility by having sex as soon as the relationship begins to "make sure" you are compatible, because you know how to predict in advance that you will be or can teach him how to please you, and (2) You can pretty much guarantee that if you can handle the emotional side of a relationship, your body is preprogrammed to take care of orgasm—regardless of whom you are with. These things being true, you can guarantee that you will never be "frigid" or force yourself into acting "like a nympho" because you are sophomorically trying to prove you can achieve orgasm if you can just find the right penis. As Shere Hite says in her famous *The Hite Report: A Nationwide Study on Female Sexuality,* "Women like sex more for the feelings involved than for the purely physical sensations of intercourse per se."

Ellis and Sagarin tell an interesting anecdote in *Nymphomania.* Their patient Eloise was a normal divorced woman, engaged to be married but secretly being sexually promiscuous. With her first husband she never really achieved orgasm, and despite all her other lovers, she only climaxed one time with one of them, and that only after she was drinking heavily.

Eloise could not endure the thought of another marriage during which she would be sexually frustrated. When Ellis questioned her, he discovered that she would only allow the missionary position, that she was turned off by anything but the most brief period of kissing and fondling, and that she encouraged the male to enter her as soon as possible, which she found mildly pleasurable. She never allowed direct clitoral stimulation. This interesting sexual predilection was the root of her problems in general, and she didn't even know it. Ellis theorizes that her lack of awareness about how her body worked and how she felt about her body and the "appropriateness" of sexual behaviors made her uncomfortable with men and eager to move the process along. Could something about your own body that *you* are blind to be preventing you from achieving intense orgasms every time? With all the *Glamour* magazine articles on the subject, with all the pop-culture emphasis on sexuality, could there be something physical we still don't know about our own bodies?

When I read the following section in *Nymphomania*, I thought perhaps I was the only woman who had never heard this. So I began asking women if they knew this interesting result of a study done in 1962. The study, conducted by those famous sex researchers Masters and Johnson, is reported in *Nymphomania* like this:

> *Anatomically, it made no sense for some females to have straight intercourse and expect to have an orgasm. For, as has recently been shown, in unusually good research by [Masters and Johnson] the female orgasm* normally results indirectly, *if not directly, from clitoral stimulation. Masters and Johnson discovered by observing females as they were actually undergoing orgasm that when the female obtains a climax during intercourse, she does so because* the inner lips of [her] genitalia penetrate sufficiently into the entrance of the vagina. *These inner lips are stimulated by the base of the penis during intercourse. When this occurs and when these inner lips of the female pull rhythmically on the clitoral region, orgasm occurs.* . . . In those cases where the inner lips are not extensive enough to enter the vaginal area, or where the penis does not pull rhythmically on them, or where they are not connected adequately with the clitoral

region, the female will almost never receive orgasm from intercourse alone *(emphasis mine)*.

Did you get that? Did you read that, ladies? Get out your mirrors! If this study is true, and there is subsequent proof that it is, for heaven's sake, get out your mirror if you don't already know how your labia are shaped.

One of the most surprising results of me telling women about this subject is that most women I spoke to didn't know we are all shaped differently. Yep, that's right. If you've seen more than one penis, you know that *they* are all shaped differently. Did you know that we are, too? Did you know that this one little fact could change your sex life forever, and not only in the most obvious way of increasing your pleasure? It can also help you choose better men because armed with this "secret" you can choose a man based on his heart and character first and his penis second. Because you can develop a loving, intimate relationship with such a man, and then since you know how your body works, you can create great sex together.

What I think the good doctors are reporting is this, in summary: Your inner lips at the top form the hood over your clitoris. If they extend all the way into your vagina, and some women's do not, chances are good that penetration will pull the lips farther into the vagina and they will massage the clitoris, thereby often giving you an orgasm from penetration. Otherwise, or in addition, by deliberate stimulation of the clitoris—by the man's tongue, his fingers, or your own fingers—you can achieve orgasm most of the time.

Most men and women I interviewed had no idea there were different physical reasons for orgasm for different women. Apparently, it isn't something people think about a whole lot, but it should be, because the ramifications are massive.

Let's walk through this whole thing. Excess sexual energy can be released through self-pleasuring—masturbation. If you know how to give yourself pleasure, you can be abstinent.

It follows that if you know your body and how it works, you can explain what you want to your lover. You don't need to "sleep around" or have sex too early in a relationship to determine if you are "compatible." In theory, you can be compatible with anyone who is willing to learn your body.

People most likely willing to learn how your body works best, and what gives you the most pleasure, are most likely to be people who love you and respect your needs. These are also the people with whom you are most likely to feel comfortable about sharing how your body works, in other words, people you know really well and care about a lot.

The Thrill of the Kill

For some people, sex is about the thrill of new beginnings. I am reminded of the woman who kept having babies because she liked babies so much and hers kept growing up. Some people spend their adult lives trying to re-create the initial feelings of the "Oh my gosh! I think I'm going to faint!" type of sexual lust/infatuation most of us have experienced at one time or another, perhaps as early as in high school.

If you have been in a long-term relationship and are reasonably objective, you can observe that even while that type of love is wonderful and thrilling and exciting, it does not last. No matter how many times you see it in movies, the truth is that pulse-altering attraction doesn't last forever. Familiarity might not only breed contempt; it also breeds, well, familiarity. If you're more in love and less in lust, that's how it's supposed to be. That's how it goes with monogamous humans. Like it or don't play the game.

Adolescent heart pounding in adults is about as far an indicator of true love as having dry spaghetti in the house is an indicator that dinner is served. Still, you can always observe some adults who mistake the first rush for the real thing and discard lots of real things because they didn't come with a crush attached. Some research indicates that the typical time infatuation lasts is six to thirty-six months, maximum. Plenty of newly married people will tell you it wanes sharply the first year, doused by the millions of little irritations that arise in living with a new person.

So what relationship value can we put on infatuation? Very, very little. Infatuation may be easy to come by for some people, but it's easy to lose for everyone.

The therapists call infatuation "projection." You take all your hopes and dreams and project them onto the other person. Like a Byzantine painting, this creates a halo effect around the person who interests you. On the screen of their personality, you project slides of whatever it is you want that person to be—and whatever you want yourself to be. Psychologists say we admire most in others those traits latent within ourselves.

Your image of the person is the image you want to create of that person, for whatever reasons you have in your head and in your past. You don't see them until the veneer wears off and the discrepancy between the almost godlike person you projected on them and the reality of their being comes crashing through. Then suddenly you begin to see the person as they truly are and can finally figure out if you really like them or if they were merely your own private viewing screen.

Therefore, another good reason to consider waiting it out before you are sexual with someone is to get beyond infatuation and projection and determine what sort of person you are dealing with. You'd then be in a much wiser position to determine if this is really someone you want to be with or not.

Let's get back to the story of Eloise, the nympho. Eloise learned about her body and suddenly her need to experiment with so many different men disappeared. She found out how to get pleasure from her relationship with her fiancé, and it was greater pleasure than any she had previously experienced. When she understood how her own body worked and shared these details with the man she loved, her roaming was annihilated, and I don't mean on her cell phone.

I think it's time for every woman to break out a mirror and take a look if they don't already have the answer to this question: Do your inner lips penetrate your vagina? If yes, you have a good chance of achieving penile-vaginal orgasm. If not, you will absolutely need clitoral stimulation. That's about all on that, except to add that simultaneously climaxing does not have to happen to have a good sex life, as long as both parties are satisfied when it's over, according to many studies. Go for the heart connection and the rest will follow.

The rationale that sex is mandatory in a new relationship just doesn't make sense. If you are going to wait until you get to know someone, you have a much better chance of being able to explain your sexuality and therefore achieve a much better time than you would if you hadn't waited and developed good communication.

Sex used to infer intimacy, connectedness, sympathy, warmth and love. It meant someone cherished you and you cherished them. It meant the person you were with was someone really, really special to you. Now we've gone so far that it's meaningless in too many instances, and we're having sex with people we scarcely know, much less love.

In *The New Celibacy,* Gabrielle Brown writes, "A kiss may indeed still be a kiss, but it's usually a promise of more to come. Without the mental script that accompanies it, a kiss is not necessarily enjoyable. If you don't agree, try being kissed at a party blindfolded, without knowing who's doing the kissing. The desire to know the giver of the kiss is far more intense than the experience of the kiss itself. . . . Sex is predominantly a mental experience . . . [and usually] also a voluntary activity.

When you end the special time you've been a BAV, do it consciously and with dignity. Honor the precious being that you are: loved and lovable, kind and worthy of respect and kindness from others. The world will pay you only as much as the price tag you put on your own life.

FIFTEEN

The Future of Sex

A lady is one who never shows her underwear unintentionally.

LILLIAN DAY, AUTHOR

To empower our children to be in control of their sexual nature, as opposed to it being in control of them, is a powerful goal for many mothers. Whatever your daughter's age, or your religious inclinations or lack thereof, there are helpful ways to discuss sexuality as a choice instead of a requirement of adolescence. How can we impart the wisdom of choice and the dignity of self-respect to our daughters? How do we give our daughters the power we have learned to wield over our own sexual nature?

Whether you are a mother now, will be some day or never will be, you have a huge responsibility as a member of female society to influence how the next generations of women will live. As we discussed earlier, your actions and example impact others even if you are unaware of it, like a drop of oil in a pot of boiling water.

Our young women are adrift now since the sexual revolution cut loose their sexual moorings. In the 1950s, we expected the majority of them to be virgins at the altar. My own father told me that my grandfather forced him to marry my mother because he had "ruined her reputation" by appearing to have had sex with her, even though they both deny to this day anything happened. We don't teach our girls that lifestyle anymore. Can we? Should we?

Remember when you were a young teen? Perhaps you tested out your ability to arouse men of any age. Remember? You flirted, you batted your eyelashes, you wore sexy clothes and occasionally made risqué comments. If you didn't do all these things, you watched other girls who did and secretly wished you could. You watched the effect women have on men and wanted to wield that power. That's part of most girls' development in our society.

It's supposed to be normal to sneak out of the house in one outfit and change into another in the girls' bathroom at school. As Rosemary Agonito asks in her 1993 book *No More "Nice Girl,"* "Don't I have anything higher to be proud of as a woman, other than my ability to be 'bad'?"

My daughter is currently entranced with a media image named Baby Spice, one of the Spice Girls. In the beginning, I simply refused to allow Spice Girl paraphernalia or music in the house, especially after I heard Sophia singing "If you wanna be my lover" on the way to elementary school. This seemed to make the Spice Girl craze all the more appealing to Sophia. Upon evaluation, I decided that *some* Spice Girl influence would be okay, balanced, appropriate. Then several members of this notorious girl band got pregnant out of wedlock.

Sophia was far too young to be having such a talk with me, but while driving to Sophia's *first-grade* class, the conversation went something like this:

SOPHIA: Mommy, the Spice Girls are pregnant.

ME: (I cringe.) Yes, I heard that.

SOPHIA: I thought you said people who aren't married couldn't get pregnant. The Spice Girls aren't married.

ME: (I take a breath.) I said people who aren't married shouldn't get pregnant. It's not the right thing to do.

SOPHIA: Do what? Do you mean have sex? (Remember, she was six at the time!)

ME: (Shocked.) Yes, having sex before you're married is wrong.

SOPHIA: Well, what is sex anyway? The fifth grader at YMCA said I would learn about it when I got to fifth grade, but I want to know now.

ME: (Unprepared to handle this with a six-year-old.) What do you think sex is, Sophie?

SOPHIA: It's when a man and a lady take off all their clothes and get in bed and kiss each other for a really long time. Then the lady has a baby.

ME: Yes, that's pretty much it, Soph. And that's only right when people are married.

SOPHIA: Is there anything else I should know about sex, Mommy?

ME: (Nearly hitting a tree.) No.

SOPHIA: That's okay because I'll learn it in fifth grade anyway and that's only, let's see (she counts on her fingers), first grade, second grade, third grade, fourth grade, fifth grade, four more grades away, right, Mommy?

I want to stop the car and tell her how wrong it is to have sex because I don't want her to be heartbroken at fourteen or pregnant at sixteen, but I fear putting into her head all the things they say make women frigid. I tell her sex is something beautiful and special to be shared by two grownups who love each other, married or not. Does she see me living this in my own life? She does now. Is it too late? Time will tell.

Today our children are taught too early way more than they need to know about how to make love and protect themselves from someone else's diseases, but they are not taught how to love—how to honor, cherish, interact with, communicate with, support, give to and receive from the opposite gender.

As we walk the schoolyard, I see little flat-chested girls in boots and miniskirts. I see bare midriffs and sexy tight skirts. I notice see-through shirts and long skirts with slits up the sides. I see moms without bras walking the kids to class. I see skintight, sexy, revealing clothing on little children. The schools are a pedophile's dream come true. How do I teach modesty without creating a weird, nerdy kid and yet instill true values and an appreciation for who she is? How do I create a Judeo-Christian set of beliefs in my child without being a Judeo-Christian person? (The church kids I grew up with were some of the wildest, so I know for a fact attendance at church guarantees nothing.)

How do we explain that dressing a certain way sends out the wrong signals when, in order to explain how those signals are received, you must impose on the child the self-consciousness of another person's possibly dirty mind? How do you instill it without instilling fear?

Dr. Rod Kennedy is a preeminent parenting expert who speaks all over the nation on excellence in parenting. He's also the father of five children and married to a middle-school principal. His must-have book, *The Encouraging Parent,* was sold by my literary agency and will be on the shelves in the spring of 2000. I asked Dr. Kennedy about sexuality. How do we train our children not to become sexual too early?

Dr. Kennedy said, "When parents ask me how to handle their children's budding interest in sex, I tell them to be open about the subject and to help their children to make healthy decisions in advance. That way, it won't be in the heat of the moment. I tell them to have their children make a contract with themselves, a contract to abstain from sex until a certain age or degree is reached. For high school or college students, that agreement might be 'I will not be sexual until I have earned my B.A.' We're not saying 'Don't have sex!' or 'Sex is bad.' What conscientious parents are saying is 'Don't engage in ignorant sex!'"

In a random sampling of mothers, I asked if they wanted their daughters to be virgins when they married. Everyone, whether she herself had or had not been a virgin, said, "No, but what we don't want is to be grandmothers while our daughters are in high

school or to have our children have to deal with the emotional
pain of failed relationships while he or she should be studying
and happy."

Dr. Kennedy said he tells his daughters, "Guys lie about love
to get sex, especially young guys." He wants his daughters to be
aware of the games, the risks and the potential for disaster inherent in being sexual too early. By frankly discussing the matter
with our daughters, perhaps introducing them to a few teenage
mothers who have an incredibly difficult life and little future,
and by encouraging them to make a commitment to themselves
to not be sexual until they reach a certain age, we are very likely
creating the optimal environment for our daughters to navigate
through their teen years.

In this age of push-up Wonderbras and show-it-all-if-you-
bend-over skirts, women are as confused as girls are. On a recent
interminable trip to a California amusement park, while waiting
for Shamu to come out of his dressing room and begin the show,
I observed the women with me in the scorching hot bleachers.

There were teenagers without bras and with spaghetti-strap
camisoles, miniskirts and shoes with three-inch-thick soles.
Their little nipples showed through cheap fabric. I'm sure not
one male in the crowd missed it.

There were, forgive me, the hausfraus. These women were
portly, wearing socks, tennis shoes and long skirts covering their
ample bottoms, usually with an inane T-shirt over the whole
miserable ensemble. They represented the opposite extreme:
Heads turned away when they occluded the horizon.

The teens were flaunting something they'd just discovered.
The hausfraus were hiding something they seemed ashamed to
own.

Surely there's a balance? Speaker, image maker and consultant Judy Jernudd describes it this way: "Princess Diana had that kind of sexiness. You knew she *would* but at the same time she projected that it wouldn't be easy. She was sexy without ever being blatant. It wasn't just what she wore, it was how she wore it that mattered."

Adult women are capable of realizing our value on the market isn't based on whether or not we look like Cindy Crawford, but our daughters are not. In her provocative and highly recommended book, *The Body Project: An Intimate History of American Girls,* Joan Jacobs Brumberg tells us the psychological and mental consequences of our cultural obsession on weight, body image, and appearance to our daughters. She says, "Until puberty, girls really are the stronger sex in terms of standard measures of physical and mental health: They are hardier, less likely to injure themselves, and more competent in social relations. But as soon as the body begins to change, a girl's advantage starts to evaporate. At that point, more and more girls begin to suffer bouts of clinical depression. The explanation of this sex difference lies in the frustrations girls feel about the divergence between their dreams for the future and the conventional sex roles implied by their emerging breasts and hips."

I am sure Brumberg offers one definite explanation for it, but could it also be that young girls begin to evaluate themselves against cultural standards for beauty and desirability and start to rank themselves against their peers in an area where winning the competition is genetic rather than mutable?

*I'm tired of all that nonsense
about beauty being only skin deep. What do
you want—an adorable pancreas?*

Jean Kerr, American author

Women need to understand the line between attractive and slutty. Since we're raising the next generation of women, I think perhaps now would be a good time to start setting the right example.

For me, one media image that comes to mind of a sexy woman who is not slutty but certainly attractively dressed is Helen Hunt's character in *Mad About You*. I had breakfast with Helen in Las Vegas in the very, very wee hours of the morning recently, and to my surprise, she manages to pull off "sexy without slutty" on the other side of the camera, too. She had just finished wrapping the last episode and was having a bit of fun, but she had that Princess Diana air about her—that "available only if you meet the criteria" thing.

And why not? Why not develop it in ourselves, and in our daughters, by teaching them how to dress and act in a modest but not dour or dowdy way? One doesn't have to be a movie star or a princess to figure out how to make that look work. It starts with two things: getting yourself a big plastic garbage bag and half a dozen women's magazines—and not the kind with the exposed breasts on the cover.

Step One: Find an image you like.

Step Two: Open up your closet.

Even if you cannot afford to replace a single garment, place in the bag everything that makes you feel slutty, ugly, dowdy, fat, stupid, dull or cheap or makes men gawk at you like you have a sign on your forehead that says, "Take me, I'm yours."

Put everything in the plastic bag and seal it tightly. Put it in the garage. From now on, wear what makes you feel good, pretty, nice, happy and feminine. Go through the magazines and find looks you like. Next time you go shopping, take the pictures of what you liked in the magazines. Even if you cannot afford the originals of the garments you see, there are bound to be knock-offs at your favorite store. Buy the best quality you can afford. Wear your new style with pride. It will do wonders for your appearance, self-image and the way you relate to men. Now when you have PMS and feel bloated, you still cannot wear grungy clothes and embarrass yourself. Once you begin taking care of your clothes and your heart (by living as a BAV), you will find you gradually begin to take better care of your body, too. Eating disorders can be modified, extra weight can be shed as you learn to like and respect yourself more.

Don't open the bag of clothes for three months. Pretend you've already given the clothes to the Salvation Army. At the end of three months, on a day you are feeling strong and proud of your new self-image, go ahead. Open the bag. You'll be shocked you were once the kind of person who would wear that stuff! Now give the clothes to charity—you know you won't miss them.

Let's teach our girls the same thing—how to dress with confidence and style without being cheap or frumpy. If you set the example and allow some modest garments but refuse to tolerate immodest ones, you will be providing your daughter with the protection she needs while a minor to guard herself against unwanted sexuality. If you explain to her that you are doing this out of love instead of to ruin her life, someday she'll grow up and thank you. I know. My parents had very strict clothing guidelines. Although I rebelled at the time, in retrospect I see it saved me a lot of pain and trouble dealing with emotional and physical entanglements I was far too young to handle.

Wendy Shalit sounds off for her generation in *A Return to Modesty* when she says that she has a strong feeling that one of the reasons relations between the sexes have come to such a painful point is precisely that the embarrassed, secretive women usually do not come forward, only the exhibitionists do. Wendy thinks that many young women now have a vastly inaccurate picture of what is normal for them to think and feel. What a painful legacy our misunderstanding of ourselves has caused these young women.

The generation before Wendy Shalit's, which is mine, grew up a bit differently. Ideally, as you matured, you accepted your sexual power as a given. After a few years of testing your charms, at last you lowered your hemline, became selective about who you tried to charm, started being more discreet. In most cases, this was part of the maturation process for young girls. You learned to modify your overt sexuality because you saw its power and its effect. Ideally, you learned how to flash it only in appropriate situations, assuming you could figure out when those appropriate situations occurred.

For women coming out of bad marriages, many of whom are as starved and gaunt inside as Nazi concentration camp survivors looked on the outside, reacclimating to the real world and reevaluating one's attractiveness take us through the whole teenage testing process again. In her book *Crazy Time*, Abigail Trafford points out how very common it is for those of us who leave particularly long-term marriages—male or female—to want to sow our wild oats.

Women and men rape and pillage as they work out their pain, or they latch onto the first thing that comes along to avoid the crazy time. However, rampant sex and hasty remarriage are poor tools for healing deep emotional pain. Yet we do it, and society supports us in this. Our movies are filled with people having sex, talking about sex, preparing to have sex. If you watch the fringe of culture, though, you'll see that our sexuality is just now entering a new stage of development: We are going from the generally acceptable idea of sleeping around (also known as "desiring wide sexual experience") to something else. The latest issue of *L.A. Weekly* talks about high school kids who think celibate is cool. There's hope for the next generation. We are moving from presuming men expect sex within a certain time period (and from dating men who really do) to recognizing that we are able to calm down our overt sexuality, and with it our blatant search mode for a mate.

Early Motherhood

Betsy got pregnant at twenty-one by a guy she had been dating only a few months. He was smoking a lot of pot and was quite unreliable as a person, although he did have a job of sorts. She knew from the first minute the relationship wasn't going anywhere, but it was easier to date him than to sit at home with her divorced mother wondering what to do on Friday nights.

Now she was carrying his baby. He flipped when she told him. Disappeared. A few weeks later, he came back and suggested they get married. She said no and kept the baby. I asked her what was going through her head when he asked her to marry him. "I just kept thinking, my baby won't have a father even if I marry this guy. I'll have two problems instead of one if I say yes."

She didn't marry him. She had the baby. She endured the demands of single motherhood with an infant. She took all the help she could get from her family. She didn't date or even think about it much. She's very content with her lifestyle now and has gone back to school to pursue her interest in graphic arts, thanks to her mother volunteering to babysit three times a week.

Leigh, who has grown sons and a young daughter, said, "I would like it if she stayed a virgin through high school. I would like that as a mother, but I don't know what she's going to be like when she's in high school, and I don't know what society will be like when she's in high school. I don't know what kind of pressure she'll be under. It's hard to say. My two older boys were sexual in their late teens—they were both in loving stable relationships when they became sexually active, and it just seemed right for them. Ideally I would like her to be a virgin until eighteen so she has the emotional maturity to be in a relationship and understand all the emotions that come with sexuality. I would love for her to have that kind of maturity. After raising two kids, I know there's a lot more they are influenced by than what their mother wishes. I'd love her to be able to handle it. They cannot handle it when they are twelve to fourteen. It could be devastating from a self-esteem issue. It's scary when you think about teen pregnancy, herpes and AIDS. At six, I won't even let her cross the street by herself. I cannot imagine her being exposed to those sorts of things."

In 1953, a quiet, rather mousy-looking zoologist named Alfred Kinsey published a book called *Sexual Behavior in the*

Human Female. It instantly became a bestseller because our culture has long been fascinated by itself. We wondered what our neighbors were doing and if they knew what we were doing. The book reported that almost 50 percent of U.S. women had engaged in sexual intercourse before marriage. Society was shocked to discover that "nice girls do!" What his heavy book of statistics did not document was the enormous sense of guilt that accompanied sexual behavior for most women and some men. Nice girls were being raised to wait until their marriage night. Apparently, at least half of them weren't listening.

Sigmund Freud popularized the idea that sexual repression was unhealthy. Freud, you will recall, had spent his early years studying mentally unstable women from high-class European families, who almost consistently reported early sexual abuse. Based on the cultural emphasis in avoiding the "dirtiness" of sex, one can easily imagine abuse was rampant in the Victorian era.

Now we have the opposite opportunity. We have nine- and ten-year-olds having sex at school. Is this any less abusive? Instead of blaming a parent in this instance, we can blame our collective society that so encourages blatant, constant sexuality that our children are being robbed of their childhoods.

In *A Return to Modesty,* Wendy Shalit reports, "Few studies that show that instruction on condom use changes the behavior of students conclude it is only likely to make them more sexually active. This cult of taking responsibility for your sexuality is essentially a call to action. . . . In a funny way, the facts about sex conceal the truth."

In *Pushing the Limits: American Women 1940-1961,* author Elaine Tyler May tells us that women of the 1950s "had to walk the difficult tightrope between sexual allure and the emphasis on virginity that permeated the youth culture." Kinsey found that half of the men he interviewed wanted to marry a virgin— although it does not appear that he asked the same question of women (whether *they* wanted to marry a virgin). Kinsey understood that this pressure to remain sexually chaste might lead to guilt and psychological disorders: "Behavior which is accepted by the culture does not generate psychological conflicts in the individual or unmanageable social problems. The same behavior, censored, condemned, tabooed or criminally punished in the next culture may generate guilt and neurotic disorders in the nonconforming individual and serious conflict within the social organism," Kinsey states.

As sex becomes conscious again instead of socially mandated, we have a real opportunity to create a utopian ideal, at least on this one front, because when sex is conscious and valued and cherished between two individuals who trust and care about one another, we will not only see a reduction in violence against women but a strengthening of the fabric of society—the family.

BAVs understand the effects of promiscuity because they have evaluated the issue. We will raise our daughters and sons to value their relationships and their sexuality. Parents or not, we accept social responsibility as forebears. We will increase the passion and fulfillment of our sexual cravings at an emotional level. We will enjoy at last true equitable union with one another.

The divorce rate could plummet, our grandchildren could be raised in happy, unbroken homes, those among us who would use celibacy or abstinence to achieve great social remedies could do so without great social stigma. The content of movies could change as our expectations of behavior change.

Closing Statement

We deal with people in clean, tidy ways and press the delete button if they get too annoying. Why not invest the time in love? Why not take time to develop true love in your life as opposed to another Internet instant message telling us we are, after all, desirable? If we are so damn desirable, if our society has given us all equal opportunity for boob jobs, good makeup, face-lifts, trendy clothes, thinner bodies, if we have all these methods of making ourselves appealing, why are we not getting the emotional results from the relationships in which we invest? Could it be that we have lost something inside in our effort to gloss up the outside? Could it be that in our rush to be popular, which should have lasted no later than high school, we sacrificed our souls on the altar of promiscuity and sanctified it by our assertion as feminists? Guess what? Blatant sexuality is not cool. Thirty years of outrageously malfunctioning society, thirty years of misery on a massive scale have finally brought in the result. As the old game show used to say, "Survey says: It's time for a change!"

The sooner we recognize the opportunity that we have to create a balanced social revolution now, the sooner we value ourselves as women, the sooner we will create for ourselves and others the opportunity to develop our true femininity. We will at last create for our daughters and ourselves the type of social factors that were the intended underpinnings of the sexual revolution in the first place. We will at last have created true equality—not the equality to screw anyone we choose at any time we choose but to create healthy, wholesome relationships based on trust, love, equality, shared interest in shared goals and shared commitments. Only when we have brought the pendulum back to center, from frigidity to promiscuity and back to conscious sexuality, will we have the opportunity to create the ideal situation between the sexes. We can believe that someday we'll be strolling down a country path hand in hand when we and our husbands are in our late seventies, white-haired and still in love, because we took the time to know and truly understand and trust the person with whom we chose to become involved.

We could have the real chance to live out our most intense and personal romantic and erotic fantasies, safe from disease, mistrust and the threat of adultery. We could bask in the hope, trust, happiness, joy, peace and even freedom that are the natural outgrowth of a life lived consciously—sexually and otherwise. We could create for ourselves and others the life we need to live, surrounded by people who love us unconditionally, supported on every side by loved ones, supported by and supportive of the community in which we live.

Becoming a BAV is replete with benefits. It is brimming over with possibilities, just like your life is now that you can see it from the new perspective of being a BAV. You and you alone can create successful, fulfilling relationships—starting with the one you have with yourself. Here's your chance. You've been sitting around wondering for the last twenty, thirty, forty years how to get what you've always wanted from life. Here's a path. You probably haven't walked this path before. Virginity in high school is not the same as born-again virginity as an adult. If your current life isn't working, what have you got to lose?

The women I interviewed for this book, and the dozens of books I have quoted, support the theory that becoming a born-again virgin is working for women all around you. Temporarily or permanently, for whatever your personal reason, a return to the virginal state is helping women figure out where they are, where they are going, who they are and who they want to become.

You have to admit, if your life was really so ideal, so close to how you want it, you wouldn't have read this far in a self-help book, would you? You would have all the men, money, free time, energy, spirituality, mental liberty and peace you possibly could want.

Long ago, so long ago I cannot attribute the quote, I read, "The world is a spinning globe, and man is a sick fly taking a dizzy ride." The only way to slow down the pace of the spinning is to jump off for a few moments and observe your behavior and that of the people around you. If you could get a macro view on your life—you know, move your brain to the wide-angle setting—what would that be worth to you? What would you do if you could look at the whole dynamic of your existence up to this point and see what works, what doesn't, and where you keep banging your head against the wall?

When you pause even for a moment and look at your own soul, surely you recognize in yourself the holy glowing seeds of how magnificent, lovely and utterly lovable you are. Surely you see how precious *your* life is and how much this world needs the contributions you have been uniquely prepared to make.

There's no real cult of the born-again virgin. A cult implies exclusivity—as in "We're saved. You're going to burn in hell." From another perspective, the inside, a cult implies to its membership that they have been set aside for a special purpose, usually by a deity. Your spiritual beliefs and the dogma you subscribe to are irrelevant to this discussion of purpose. Every religion and spiritual belief is essentially the same at its core. "Love others and do what you're supposed to do" are the basis of all belief systems. Actually those two beliefs are one and the same. By doing what you are supposed to do (with your life, your day, your thoughts, your body) you *are* loving others in a literal and existential way.

If this is true, then it is reasonable to assume that whatever higher power you do or don't believe in, you have a purpose in this life. That could mean you are the only efficient checker at Wal-Mart or it could mean you are the next Mother Teresa. Only you know what that purpose is.

Dear sister, in the frenzy we create in our lives by running after men or sexual gratification, we amplify the insanity. While this is not the only way we create background noise that drowns out the pleas of our soul, it is the most obvious and easy one to deal with. Perhaps by finding access to the still, quiet voice within you, you can further manifest your greatness. You are special, you are precious, you are worthy of being loved and praised. When you know this about yourself, you will be ready to wield your own internal power—the magical self-power of the strong, true, wise women who are members of the cult of the born-again virgin.

Every blessing to you, my sister!

Bibliography

Adams, Abby. *An Uncommon Scold.* New York: Simon & Schuster, 1989.

Agonito, Rosemary. *History of Ideas on Women: A Sourcebook.* New York: Perigee, 1978.

———. *No More "Nice Girl": Power, Sexuality and Sex in the Workplace.* Holbrook, MA: B. Adams, Inc., 1993.

Avery, Gillian. *Victorian People in Life and Literature.* New York: Holt, Rinehart & Winston, 1970.

The Bible: New American Standard Version. Cambridge, England: Cambridge University Press, 1977.

Bingham, Caroline. *The Stewart Kingdom of Scotland, 1371–1603.* New York: St. Martin's Press, 1975, 1974.

Brumberg, Joan Jacobs. *The Body Project: An Intimate History of American Girls.* New York: Random House, 1997.

Brown, Gabrielle. *The New Celibacy.* New York: McGraw Hill, 1980.

Cameron, Julia, with Mark Bryan. *The Artist's Way.* New York: Tarcher/Putnam, 1992.

Carroll, Doug. "In Search of Intimacy," *Arizona Republic,* February 14, 1999.

———. "Why I'm Committed to Being Celibate," *Arizona Republic,* February 14, 1999.

Clinton, Hillary Rodham. *It Takes a Village: And Other Lessons Children Teach Us.* New York: Simon & Schuster, 1996.

Cowan, Connell, and Melvyn Kinder. *Smart Women, Foolish Choices: Finding the Right Men and Avoiding the Wrong Ones.* New York: C. N. Potter, 1985.

De Angelis, Barbara. *Real Moments for Lovers.* New York: Delacorte Press, 1995.

Donaldon, Gordon. *Scottish Kings.* New York: John Wiley, 1967.

Ellis, Albert, and Edward Sagarin. *Nymphomania: A Study of the Oversexed Woman.* New York: Gramercy Publishing, 1964.

Engels, Friedrich, and Michele Barrett. *The Origin of the Family, Private Property and the State, in the Light of the Researches of Lewis H. Morgan, with an Introduction and Notes by Eleanor Burke Leacock.* New York: International Publishers, 1972, 1942.

Erickson, Carolly. *The First Elizabeth.* New York: Summit Books, 1983.

Fein, Ellen and Sherrie Schneider. *The Rules.* New York: Warner Books, 1995.

Frankl, Viktor. *Man's Search for Meaning: An Introduction to Logotherapy.* New York: Washington Square Press, 1946.

Fraser, Antonia. *Mary, Queen of Scots,* New York: Delacorte Press, 1969.

———. *The Weaker Vessel.* New York: Alfred A. Knopf, 1984.

———. *The Warrior Queens: The Legends and the Lives of the Women Who Have Led Their Nations in War.* New York: Alfred A. Knopf, 1989.

———. *The Wives of Henry VIII.* New York: Alfred A Knopf, 1992.

Friedan, Betty. *The Feminine Mystique.* New York: Norton, 1963.

Fromm, Erich. *Love, Sexuality and Matriarchy: About Gender,* edited and with an introduction by Rainer Funk. New York: Fromm International, 1997.

Gray, John. *Men Are from Mars, Women Are from Venus: A Practical Guide to Improving Communication and Getting What You Want in Your Relationships.* New York: HarperCollins, 1992.

Hansen, Mark Victor, and Jack Canfield. *Chicken Soup for the Soul* (series). Deerfield Beach, Fla.: Health Communications, Inc., 1993 ff.

Hansen, Mark Victor. *Living Your Dreams,* sound recording, Newport Beach, Calif.: MVH & Associates, 1999.

Hill, Napoleon. *Think and Grow Rich.* Cleveland: The Ralston Society, 1947.

Hite, Shere. *The Hite Report: A Nationwide Study on Female Sexuality.* New York: Macmillan, 1976.

Hume, Martin. *The Courtships of Queen Elizabeth: A History of the Various Negotiations for Her Marriage.* New York: McClure, Phillips & Co., 1906 (out of print).

Jakubowski, Patricia, and Arthur Lange. *Assertive Option: Your Rights and Responsibilities.* Atlanta: Research Press, 1978.

Jeffers, Susan. *Opening Our Hearts to Men.* New York: Fawcett Columbine, 1989.

Jenkins, Elizabeth. *Elizabeth the Great.* New York: Coward-McCann, Inc., 1958 (out of print).

Johnson, Robert A. *We: Understanding the Psychology of Romantic Love.* San Francisco: Harper San Francisco, 1983.

Kennedy, Roderick. *The Encouraging Parent.* New York: Times Books, 1999.

Kinsey, Alfred C., with the staff of the Institute for Sex Research, Indiana University. *Sexual Behavior in the Human Female.* Philadelphia: Saunders, 1953.

Margolis, Char, with Victoria St. George. *Questions from Earth, Answers from Heaven.* New York: SMP, 1999.

Martin, Iris. *From Couch to Corporation.* New York: John Wiley & Sons, 1996.

Maslow, Abraham H. *Motivation and Personality.* New York: Harper and Row, 1970.

Maslow, Abraham H., and Richard Lowry. *Toward a Psychology of Being.* New York: John Wiley & Sons, 1998.

Masters, William H., Robert C. Kolodny, and Virginia E. Johnson. *On Sex and Human Loving.* Boston: Little, Brown & Co., 1988.

May, Elaine Tyler. *Pushing the Limits: American Women 1940–1961.* London: Oxford University Press, 1998.

Montagu, Ashley. *The Natural Superiority of Women.* New York: Macmillan, 1952, 1953, 1954, 1968.

Morrisson, N. Brysson. *Mary Queen of Scots.* London: Vista Books, 1960.

Norris, Kathleen. *The Cloister Walk.* New York: Riverhead Books, 1996.

Powell, Elizabeth. *Talking Back to Sexual Pressure: What to Say.* Minneapolis, Minn.: CompCare Publishers, 1991.

Robbins, Anthony. *Personal Power*, sound recording. Irwindale, Calif.: Robbins Research Int'l., 1989.

————. *Awaken the Giant Within: How to Take Immediate Control of Your Mental, Emotional, Physical and Financial Destiny.* New York: Summit Books, 1991.

Ruiz, Don Miguel. *The Four Elements: A Toltec Wisdom Book.* San Rafael, Calif.: Amber-Allen Publishing, 1997.

Saint Benedict. *The Rule of the Master: Regule Magistri,* Luke Eberle, ed. Kalamazoo, Mich.: Cistercian Publications, 1977.

Schlessinger, Laura C. *Ten Stupid Things Women Do to Mess Up Their Lives.* New York: Villard Books, 1994.

Segal, Lynne. *Is the Future Female? Troubled Thoughts on Contemporary Feminism.* New York: P. Bedrick Books, 1988, 1987 (out of print).

Shalit, Wendy. *A Return to Modesty: Discovering the Lost Virtue.* New York: Free Press, 1999.

Shouson, George Malcolm. *The Crimes of Mary Stuart.* New York: E.P. Dutton & Co., Inc., 1967.

Smith, Cynthia S. *Why Women Shouldn't Marry.* Boston: Lyle Stuart Inc., 1988.

Steinem, Gloria. *Revolution from Within: A Book of Self-Esteem.* Boston: Little, Brown & Co., 1992.

Swami Prabhupada, A.C. Bhaktivendanta. *Bhagavad-Gita: As It Is.* New York: The Bhaktivendanta Book Trust, 1968.

Tao Teh Ching: A New English Version. New York: HarperPerennial, 1992.

Tingsten, Herbert. *Victoria and the Victorians.* New York: Delacorte, 1965, 1972 (out of print).

Tracy, Brian. *The Psychology of Achievement,* sound recording. Chicago: Nightingale-Conant Corp., 1984.

Trafford, Abigail. *Crazy Time: Surviving Divorce and Building a New Life.* New York: HarperPerennial, 1993.

Warschaw, Tessa Albert. *Rich Is Better: How Women Can Bridge the Gap Between Wanting and Having It All: Financially, Emotionally, Professionally.* New York: Signet Books, 1986.

Weintraub, Stanley. *Victoria: Biography of a Queen.* London: Unwin Paperbacks, 1987.

Westheimer, Ruth, and Louis Lieberman. *Sex and Morality: Who Is Teaching Our Sex Standards?* Boston: Harcourt Brace Jovanovich, 1988.

Williams, Donna Marie. *Sensual Celibacy.* New York: Fireside, 1999.

Wolfe, Leanna. *Women Who May Never Marry: The Reasons, Realities and Opportunities.* Atlanta: Longstreet Press, Inc., 1995.

Wollstonecraft, Mary A. *Vindication of the Rights of Women,* 1792 (out of print).

———. *Ahead of Her Time: A Sampler of Life and Thoughts of Mary Wollstonecraft,* Ella Mazel, ed. London, Brighton, New York, Philadelphia, Singapore: Brunner/Mazel Inc.,1996.

Young, G. M. *Victorian England: Portrait of an Age.* London: Oxford University Press, 1936, 1967.

Index

Author Information

To book Wendy as a speaker
Or to
Speak to Wendy about your book,
Her book,
Or any of her clients' books,
Contact:

ForthWrite Literary Agency
& Speaker's Bureau
23852 West Pacific Coast Highway
No. 701
Malibu, CA 90265

email queries preferred: *VirginCult@aol.com*

A New Season of
Chicken Soup for the Soul

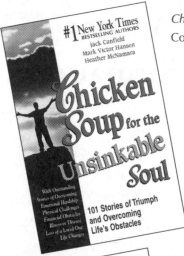

Visionary Fiction from HCI

Wings of Destiny

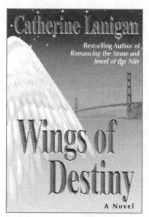

Catherine Lanigan, best-selling author of *Romancing the Stone* and *Jewel of the Nile*, returns with a sweeping tale centered on the courage and irrepressible spirit of its protagonist heroine. The story of Jefferson Duke, who sacrifices the most precious of life's gifts: his heart and his granddaughter Barbara, who must betray him and, ultimately, learn the truth about herself and her own secret past.

Code #6900 Hardcover • $24.00

Rings of Truth

A profound tale of a man's journey to discover his true self. Matt, a motivational speaker, has it all, until a spiritual apparition allows him to see that his material success means nothing if his soul is empty. Follow him on his transformative journey of awareness and awakening as he develops a greater understanding of who he his and teaches those around him, one truth at a time.

Code #7249 Paperback • $12.95

WOMEN AND HEART DISEASE
A GROUNDBREAKING BOOK!

The first to recognize that heart disease is the most serious killer of women in the United States.

Code #6935 Paperback • $10.95

A moving, first-person account of one woman's journey through a life-threatening heart attack, the physical and emotional roller-coaster ride directly following the attack, her rehabilitation, her ongoing efforts to reverse heart disease, and, especially, her commitment to reclaiming her life and re-creating her self-image.

It is a candid and intimate portrait, and a testament to the courage and faith necessary to successfully undertake a journey of healing, the magnitude of which inevitably results in self-transformation.

THOUGHTS TO LIVE BY

The graceful, remarkable words in this inspiring collection are filled with purity and love. In our fast-paced world, filled with turmoil and tragedy, the simple and gentle wisdom of the *Kiss of God* is sure to make it a treasured favorite.

Code # 7435 Paperback • $9.95

Code 7230 Paperback • $6.95

A unique gem of a book, overflowing with profound truths that will help you find meaning and understanding in a sometimes difficult world.

Pearls of Wisdom will guide you to live each day with an open heart.

The Love of Knowledge

Code #7206—$10.95

From its birth in ancient Greece to the present day, philosophy has inspired us with insightful questions and thoughts to help us live life to the fullest.

This book will give you the basic tenets for many of the most important thinkers throughout history and show you how they relate directly to our everyday life. From advertising slogans to celebrities, to familiar phrases, you'll be amazed at how much of our popular culture results from the teachings of the great philosophers.